# FORTUNES & BLUNDERS

5 MONEY LESSONS FROM THE RICH AND FAMOUS

DAVID SCHNEIDER

DAVID SCHNEIDER

Copyright © 2018 by David Schneider. All rights reserved.
Published by Writingale Publishing, LLC

No part of this book may be reproduced in any form or by any electronic or mechanical means, including information storage and retrieval systems, without written permission from the authors, except in the case of a reviewer, who may quote brief passages embodied in critical articles or in a review. Trademarked names appear throughout this book. Rather than use a trademark symbol with every occurrence of a trademarked name, names are used in an editorial fashion, with no intention of infringement of the respective owner's trademark.

Although the author and publisher have made every effort to ensure that the information in this book was correct at press time, the authors and publisher do not assume and hereby disclaim any liability to any party for any loss, damage, or disruption caused by errors or omissions, whether such errors or omissions result from negligence, accident, or any other cause. The information in this book is distributed on an "as is" basis, without warranty. Although every precaution has been taken in the preparation of this work, neither the authors nor the publisher shall have any liability to any person or entity with respect to any loss or damage caused or alleged to be caused directly or indirectly by the information contained in this book. The material contained herein is not investment advice. Individuals should carefully research their own investment decisions and seek the advice of a registered financial planner where appropriate.

Writingale Publishing also publishes its books in a variety of electronic formats. For more information about Writingale Publishing products, visit our Website at www.thewritingale.com.

ISBN-13: 978-1-727-70807-3

First Edition: October 2018

# CONTENTS

Introduction ..................................................................... 1
**PART ONE Ten Lives** .................................................. 8
Chapter 1 THE ORIGINAL INFLUENCERS ...................... 10
Chapter 2 STARS FROM HOLLYWOOD ......................... 36
Chapter 3 SPORTING ICONS .......................................... 57
Chapter 4 LATIN AMERICAN TYCOONS ....................... 81
Chapter 5 RUSSIAN OLIGARCHS .................................. 104
**PART TWO Lessons Learned** ................................... 135
Chapter 6 ON GENERAL SUCCESS AND FAILURE ...... 137
Chapter 7 FIVE MONEY LESSONS ................................ 151
Conclusions ................................................................. 164
Afterword .................................................................... 168
Thank You ................................................................... 170
Acknowledgements .................................................... 171
About the Author ........................................................ 172
More from the Author ................................................ 173

# Introduction

## *The Money Challenge*

Nothing defines us more than the decisions we make in our lives, from the spur of the moment decision to the execution of a well-calculated plan that could reach years into the future. It shapes our destinies, our successes, and our failures in life. And nothing is more fascinating than to go back to those decisions that define these life-changing moments.

Arguably the toughest decisions in life are about money, how we make it, and how we can keep it and even grow it. Whether we like it or not, money dominates our lives. Consider all the consumer goods and services we crave throughout our lives—smartphones, clothes, cars and travel. There is not much that does not require money. Often, we define success based on how much money we make or how much a person's net worth is. The decisions we have to make in this regard are not always easy. In fact, they can be nerve-racking. Yet, so little is done to improve our financial knowledge. So little is taught in our education systems, starting from elementary school and right through to university. We are reluctant to discuss the subject even with our families. Talking about money is frowned upon—having is not—but how can we maximize our financial potential?

It's a common problem throughout different generations, gender and social classes; worldwide, throughout history, it's the same pattern over and over again. This is astonishing considering that making and managing money is arguably one of the most fundamental responsibilities in our lives. At least to most of us. And if you are reading this book, I am guessing that it is to you as well—from investing in your education to planning your retirement.

### *The Wrong Role Models*

In recent years, thanks to free media and the internet, more and more of us have sought to familiarize ourselves with the personalities from Wall Street and money successes. Many good personalities have emerged, but so have a number of bad.

Our first instinct is to look at people who are professional money managers, those who manage billions of dollars for others day in and day out. When we watch Bloomberg or CNBC, we see Ivy League-trained MBA money managers, men and women who move billions of dollars with a push of a button. They speak in a language that sounds distant and unfamiliar to most of us—in a language that is alien to us. I would argue that the knowledge and wisdom they proclaim has very limited application to the average Joe, those without finance degrees or special sales training.

Then there are the stars of Wall Street (those Masters of the Universe). Hedge fund managers, such as George Soros, Paul Singer or Ray Dalio. Among investors, day traders and those who who strive to be either one they have become modern-day heroes. But frankly, what can we learn from a person who manages billions for others? What can we learn about their macro-trading strategies, elaborate hedging operations, and the mind-boggling financial leverage they deploy every single day?

I admit that no one has taught me more about money and investing than Warren Buffett, his mentor Benjamin Graham, and his business partner Charlie Munger. Just reading their publications and seeing their interviews beat any training in commercial banking or a degree in finance. But as fascinating as their financial lives might be, the lessons we can learn from them are, to be honest, limited. Not everyone can be like Warren Buffett or Charlie Munger: rational, intellectually superior, and without any obvious character flaws. Not everyone can follow the mechanical ways of investing that Benjamin Graham practiced.

There is also a new breed of money management. This is a trend towards computerized and fully automated trading and money management. These new masters are physics and mathematics PhDs; they are (sometimes literally) rocket scientists. This new trend has also manifested itself in retail money management. Firms such as Betterment Investment or Wealthfront offer fully automated investment management products. But even simple index funds and ETFs offered by giant asset managers such as BlackRock and Vanguard illustrate the new trend. Money management has become faceless, passing over responsibilities to computer programs and fast trading executions. Have you ever heard of Gerry O'Reilly? A man who commands $800 billion in assets at Vanguard's Index Fund operations.[1] According to a Bloomberg interview, he makes sure that every trading day the $450 billion Vanguard Total Stock Market Index Fund matches the performance of its 3,600-stock benchmark. Yet, it is a name that not even the most fervent Vanguard client and fan has ever heard of.

But what can we learn from highly technical computer models that automatically make, buy, and sell decisions in a fraction of a second? Algorithmic (Algo) trading strategies, double butterfly option with delta 0.5 and implied volatility of 15%—tested through Monte Carlo simulation or intricate VAR correlations —not much! There is certainly something good about this trend—lower fees and more transparency—but the learning value for us as individuals is virtually zero, unless we count transferring our money on a monthly basis using a standing order as a learning experience.

Then, there are the new financial heroes of social media. Who doesn't know about TV personalities like James Cramer, as his relentless rants on CNBC seem to pop up every minute, or James Altucher, who lives in a pseudo-world of financial fantasies and make believe. You can see his face appear on virtually any money website promoting bizarre-sounding trading strategies and the new wealth in Bitcoin and other cryptocurrencies. He is giving snake oil businessmen a new face—curly hair with spectacles and a gangly upper body.

Many of these money leaders entertain just through their outrageousness. Unfortunately, humans, with strong herd instinct, tend to go for the individuals who scream the loudest or make the most outrageous claims—many times with fatal consequences. Follow them at your own peril.

Like anything in life, choosing the right role models is not easy, especially when it comes to handling money.

### *A Love for Biographies*

I have always been a great fan of biographies of famous and inspirational people. Even in elementary school, I read the short biographies found in the children's section at my local library.

Something that still stands out from my childhood is the works of Plutarch. Even the old Romans adored and devoured Plutarch's Lives of the Noble Greeks and Romans, commonly called Parallel Lives or Plutarch's Lives. It is probably one of the few book collections that has captivated generations, and will continue to captivate generations to come.

Today, I still love reading and listening to audiobooks that describe the lives of famous and successful people. Names such as Jeff Bezos, Steve Jobs, and even Donald Trump. Particularly, US Americans are familiar with the lives of Benjamin Franklin or Abraham Lincoln. In most living rooms of middle class America you can find a copy of these biographies on the bookshelves. At home, I have a collection of biographies ranging from Otto von Bismarck, first Chancellor of the German Empire between 1871 and 1890, to Richard Branson's autobiography, Finding My Virginity.

Biographies of famous and powerful people can inspire us, teach us worldly wisdom, and entertain us. Biographies are not abstract like many academic books. They are more entertaining than most "how to" books. They present real-life experiences that range from pure drama to unbelievably lucky breaks. Biographies certainly can captivate the reader by presenting vivid examples of their subject's lives—whether in good or bad times. And they contain lessons—numerous, very powerful lessons.

What does learning about money have to do with the lives of the rich and famous?

Love them or not, most of us are fascinated by the rich and famous. We follow celebrities on Instagram, Twitter, and other social media. We follow every step and every move they make. We are in awe of their success, but we are even more amused by their failures. Gossip magazines are filled with their private blunders, affairs, and in some cases, dramatic career endings. Surprisingly, we actually learn very little from them, especially when it comes to the topic of money.

This book addresses the problem we have with money. It tackles the learning that we need to maximize our potential, and does so by looking at the lives of those who often have the most…and can lose the most.

In this book, we will study the lives of the rich and famous; we will learn about and analyze the lives of 10 personalities—each one having their own interesting story to tell and lessons to teach us when it comes to the matter of making, maintaining and (occasionally) losing their fortunes.

### The Structure of the Book

This book is structured into two parts. The first part contains the biographies of 10 rich and/or famous people. I have grouped the subjects in pairs, usually with similar backgrounds, era, generation or profession. In order to highlight the stark contrasts in the examples, I will explore a good and a bad example for each pair. By contrasting their strengths and weaknesses, we might be able to draw our own conclusions more easily. At the end of each chapter, I will contrast both examples to support us in our quest for learning.

In the second part, I summarize all findings from Part I by grouping them into key lessons learned, successes and failures. Lessons that include actionable advice and focus on important aspects of money management that might ultimately impact our lives.

Some of the outcomes seem like just common sense and others might surprise you, but all are valuable. So, sit back and experience the battle of the rich and famous as they seek to become our personal role models that might guide us to our own financial stardom.

### Get Your Bonus Chapter

If you are interested in reading the bonus chapter about Middle Eastern wealth and blunders, subscribe to my email list. More details will follow at the end of the book.

DAVID SCHNEIDER

# PART ONE
# TEN LIVES

## Chapter 1
# THE ORIGINAL INFLUENCERS

We can find many examples of financial successes and economic blunders over the centuries, from the great Emperors of Rome, Egypt and China to the Wall Street Crash and the Great Depression. Wealthy people becoming bankrupt overnight.

Circumstances beyond the control of its victims. Consider being a wealthy German during the Second World War, when an entire fortune might be needed to buy an 8 million mark stamp. On other occasions, events take place beyond the control of the individual. Imagine being a Jew in Europe during the same Nazi period. Not just your home, your business, your wealth might disappear in a flash, but also your life.

To have resonance for life in the 21st century, we really need to concentrate no further back than a century ago. Since the days of the great men to follow, we have seen global changes in the world's finances. Nevertheless, the financial stories of Winston Churchill and John Maynard Keynes can provide us with many lessons. These two may have been great thinkers, but were they great at managing their money?

*John Maynard Keynes—The Money Condor*

*"Most men love money and security more, and creation and construction less, as they get older."—John Maynard Keynes*

How many fortunes do you need to lose to learn a lesson? One, two? Or is the lesson one that tells us the risk never goes away? At least, for speculators in the financial markets? John Maynard Keynes made use of his own experience—his successes and failures—to develop his theory of economics. Keynesian economics underpins the work of governments around the world, even today, now more than seventy years after his death.

Many consider him the greatest economist of all time—certainly, his thinking has shaped the lives of those from the developed world. He is considered the creator of modern macroeconomics, building the foundations for the school of thought known as Keynesian economics. Among investors, he is also regarded as an early "value investor" and forefather of behavioral economics, a branch of economics that has gained mainstream popularity in recent years. His influence in these fields has stood the test of time for generations.

But it wasn't only astounding professional career achievements or his lasting works from his academic life that can teach us lessons, but also his astonishing personal achievements when it came to accumulating his private wealth—several times! As such, it would be easy to assume that Keynes was as successful with his own finances as he was in informing those of the nations of the world. And while that is a truth we can ultimately reach, Keynes' journey to personal wealth was far from smooth. He faced many challenges, some of his own making, some out of his control.

At Keynes's death, in 1946, his net worth was estimated at

£500,000. That is a personal fortune worth close to $7 million in 2018. On top of this, his personal and extensive collection of artwork and rare manuscripts are valued at more than $2 million. Pretty impressive for a man who, as we shall see, grew up during times of considerable economic turbulence, who lived through two world wars and the biggest financial collapse in the history of the world, and whose own life reflected the most stereotypical of British middle-class values. In other words, an elaborate lifestyle supported by unexceptional means.

Keynes' collection of assets was impressive. Not only did it include his extensive stock portfolio, but also an elaborate paper written by Sir Isaac Newton, rare books, and paintings. But although a monetary value can be applied to these wonders, it is their intrinsic worth that makes them so remarkable. As a connoisseur of fine art and writing of lasting importance, Keynes always had an eye for the best.

In his collection were not only several pieces by Cubists George Braque and Pablo Picasso (Picasso was in his outer circle of friends) and other famous artists of that time, but he also acquired the original manuscript of Principia Mathematica and other papers of Isaac Newton. He also owned rare classic books by Aristotle, St. Augustine, Bacon, Copernicus, Dryden, Galileo, Hobbes, Erasmus, Kepler, Milton, More, and Virgil, as well as First Editions of Milton's Paradise Lost, Spenser's The Faerie Queen, and Ben Jonson's plays.[2]

How did he garner such an impressive and valuable collection? Along with his personal wealth, his private stockpile of valuable works of art and papers made him, according to John F. Wasik, author of Keynes's Way to Wealth, Keynes was one of the richest economists ever.[3]

### *Keynes' Formative Years*

John Maynard Keynes, later the 1st Baron Keynes, was born June 5th, 1883 in Cambridge, England, to an upper middle-class family. Despite their comfortable background, supplies of cash within the household were limited. Certainly, the family lived nowhere near the poverty line, but compared to the vast wealth held by a small number of the middle, upper and emerging classes in Victorian Britain, their finances were of no particular note. His father, John Neville Keynes, was an economist and a lecturer in moral sciences at the University of Cambridge, and his mother, Florence Ada Keynes, was a local social reformer. Their son's later good works and support for important causes may well have had its origins in such socially-aware parents. John Maynard Keynes himself would be destined to follow an appropriate educational route for his social standing and class, but one earned through scholarship (a reward for academic brilliance) rather than family funding.

Coming from an upper middle-income family of learned academics, he received the best education England had to offer at that time: firstly Eton College and then Cambridge, both entered through scholarships in 1897 and 1902, respectively. He excelled in both, and early on showed his talent for analytical and intellectual brilliance. According to biographers, he particularly displayed a talent for mathematics, although he also demonstrated a keen interest in classics and history as well.

In line with his education, he took the national civil service exam in 1906 to serve his country in some form of administrative role. He would have been unusual for that time in possessing considerable academic talent as well as the correct breeding and schooling. High intelligence and social awareness were not characteristics especially associated with the British Civil Service in the immediate post-Victorian years. He took a position in the India office, although he didn't have much interest in India. However, the British Raj held complete rule at the time, and the position gave him key insights into how money worked in society and its importance to the functioning of civilization. It was hardly a glamorous job, though: Keynes's first task in the office was to ship ten Ayrshire bulls to Bombay.

Nevertheless, he developed a keen interest in macroeconomics, the big picture form of economics that includes the analysis of capital flows, currency and government policies related to industry and economics. With that, he also developed a deep interest in probability calculation that often connected with macroeconomic decision-making. So interested was he in this subject, that one of his first books published would be on probability theory.[4]

After two years of being a small-time civil servant, he got bored and looked for new challenges. He returned to Cambridge in 1908, where King's College offered him the position of second bursar. It was clear that a future in economics, following in his father's footsteps, was in the cards. In time, he would eclipse the work of his parent.

### *Keynes' Work and Income*

In his personal life, Keynes demonstrated the same drive that would come to epitomize his career as an economist. He early on showed a strong determination to achieve personal freedom—to enjoy a life he had always envisioned for himself, surrounded by friends and fellow intellectuals. He was not averse as well to sexual stimulation. These were ambitions often beyond those of a simple academic or burgeoning intellectual of his time.

But behind everything was the small matter of money. Keynes mixed with people who had, to put it bluntly, plenty. Remember, he was educated at Eton, which in those days was a school for the very rich and the very privileged (some might say it still is, although the scholarships and bursaries it now offers open up its unique kind of education to a wider selection of society). From there, it was Cambridge, itself a hotbed of advantage at the turn of the twentieth century, and finally into one of the only two or three options for "gentlemen" of the era. If personal wealth was not quite sufficient to enable a life of sport and play without work, then the army or the civil service were the career routes of the rich. Keynes was of this social group in every way except in his own finances.

Keynes didn't inherit wealth. At first, his financial resources were limited. He had to rely on his small allowances and his meager salary from Cambridge. According to one biographer, he was dependent upon allowances (roughly $160 each) from his father and his mentor, Alfred Marshall.

His first official salaried income came when he served as a civil servant in the India Office. When he returned to full-time academic functions in 1908, he would earn income from lecturing and tutoring; included here were stints at London School of Economics and, later, a return to his alma mater, Cambridge.

With each passing year, his reputation grew, so the salary and fees he could command increased. Keynes might have matched his peers' wealth by now, but he did this through hard work and considerable talent. His finances were not based on inheritance from wealthy relatives.

As was expected of any high-ranking academic, Keynes published his first article in 1909. It appeared in The Economic Journal and took as its subject matter the effect of a recent global economic downturn on India. This would lead to recognition and consequently to more opportunities. On being elected a fellow in 1911, Keynes was made editor of the same periodical as had published his first work. His lecturing, private tutoring and finally his position as Bursar at a Cambridge University would help him steadily increase his income—something that would continue until the outbreak of World War I.

However, by themselves, neither his salary nor his lecturing fees were able to move him into the category of the super-rich (which he later achieved). It was his understanding of economics that drove his success. The money world made sense to him in a way that it did to few others. On top of this, his ability to share his knowledge in a way that made it understandable to others turned him into a household name—and a very wealthy one at that. It was these skills that accelerated his earnings and gave him the ability to withstand (as Shakespeare might have said) the "slings and arrows of outrageous (economic) fortune."

The first book he published was the interestingly titled Indian Currency and Finance. Published in 1913, it wasn't, admittedly, the Harry Potter of its day. Neither was it his first nor only book project, however. Nevertheless, it served its purpose, as the British government took note of this young, talented man.

With the outbreak of the First World War, Keynes elevated to a position of national economic influence. The British Government sought men with expertise in money, currencies, and finance to handle payments for materials. The day of the well-brought-up but not terribly able amateur was coming to an end. In the time of war, the position of world dominance the British had enjoyed during the Victorian era was under severe threat. The time for playing at economics was over.

Keynes' book, Indian Currency and Finance, demonstrated his talent for writing and his deep understanding of the subject matter that was valuable to the British government.[5] Keynes was appointed to a government commission at the Treasury, a position which he would hold from 1915 until 1919.

When World War I ended, he was assigned to advise the Treasury on the Versailles Treaty, but he vehemently disagreed with the reparations that were being extracted from Germany. Based on his knowledge of exports, currency, and industrial production, he believed that Germany would be economically crushed by what France, Britain, and the United States were demanding. It was, of course, that economic straightjacket that created the circumstances through which Adolf Hitler would be able to rise to power.

Unable to come to terms with the sanctions imposed by the victorious nations in the immediate aftermath of the First World War, he left his post and began writing another book. It was one that would change both his career and foreign policy forever.

This book was called The Economic Consequences of the Peace and was published in 1919. His book became an instant bestseller on both sides of the Atlantic, and he morphed into the contemporary equivalent of a superstar. Unfortunately, not without some repercussions at home.

Publishing this book, with such an obvious title, was an enormous career risk that demonstrated that Keynes wasn't afraid to make decisions based on possibly personally disadvantageous outcomes. He openly criticized the same people for whom he worked, and he would forever make enemies in the ranks of powerful politicians and popular thinkers of that time. But his daring endeavor paid off. By polarizing the audience and openly challenge the existing status quo, Keynes drew attention to his work. It certainly helped him with his future publishing career.

There can be no doubt that this latest book represented Keynes' big break. This was in terms of increased income and fame, as well as the self-perpetuating circle of increased income increased recognition brings. It would not only boost his already successful career as academic, lecturer and author, but to this he would add income from being a journalist (he also became in demand as a journalist, writing for The Nation, the Manchester Guardian, and The New Republic), and highly sought-after speaker.

In turn, it opened up commercial opportunities. One proposal was to chair a foreign-owned bank. He turned it down. His friend Oswald "Foxy" Falk, an impetuous stockbroker who worked in the City, secured an invitation for Keynes to join the board of the National Mutual Life Assurance Society, which he accepted.

From 1921 through 1938, Keynes served as chairman of the gigantic Insurance Company. Another stable and not inconsiderable income stream fed his bank account. As much as it might have been frowned upon by the circles in which his parents had aspired to inhabit, Keynes began to develop an increasing reputation in the commercial world. He began to play the stock markets, investing the money of others but not afraid of a dabble himself.

Once more, Keynes demonstrated his enormous capacity to

learn. He was never a man to feel he had reached the zenith of his field, and that, of course, was a major reason why he did make it to the top of economics, not just nationally but in global terms. That lesson of never ceasing to learn, especially from one's mistakes, is applicable in all fields of endeavor.

### *Keynes Budgeting and Spending Habits*

Prior to the success of The Economic Consequences of the Peace, Keynes lived modestly (certainly not as well as he would have liked) compared to normal expectations for a member of his class. There are no records that Keynes overspent egregiously, gambled lavishly or had to borrow for a luxurious lifestyle inappropriate for his financial income at any point of his lifetime. After all, he was his own accountant, keeping track of income and expenses in a personal ledger from an early age.

Nevertheless, as his income grew, so did his propensity to indulge in la dolce vita.[6] As his income increased, so did his expenditures. He always had a taste for the good life, seeking out experience and cultural education. For example, even during his relatively impoverished, pre-First World War days, he would take regular vacations, visiting Greece, Sicily, Italy, and France. He played golf, gambled at Monte Carlo (but not excessively and there are no records of massive losses unlike, for example, Churchill—whom we will visit later), and started collecting books and art in earnest. But it was always appropriate spending relative to his earning power, and he never accumulated excessive debt by borrowing money for things he shouldn't or couldn't afford. Besides, as you can see from his private collection of art and writings, he had a keen eye for enduring value.

After his success with The Economic Consequences of the Peace in 1919, profits from his books and his teaching income allowed him to live the life of an aristocrat, even though he was still early in his academic and writing career. In support of his investment in art, he traveled to the Continent and picked up Impressionist masterpieces for a song after 1919. He enjoyed collecting books, acquiring and protecting many of Isaac Newton's papers. In part, on the basis of these papers, Keynes described Newton as "the last of the magicians."[7]

He finally reached the stage of having more money than he could easily spend, leaving him with considerable disposable income.

## *Keynes the Speculator*

Risk taking was always part of Keynes' life. The specific risks he took would crystalize themselves in two different ways: writing and speculation in the markets. This risk-taking element was in part a wish to increase his wealth. But it was also a part of his personality. His student and first biographer, Roy Harrod, noted that "by temperament, he was courageous and always ready to take risks . . . one who had managed the external finances of the nation during the war would surely have some market value in the world of finance."[8]

Speculating in the financial markets came naturally. Early on as an academic, he took it on as an intellectual challenge with the added benefit of making some income—so he thought. Money was in short supply, after all, in the early days. The notion of making and losing a fortune was, indeed, a very romantic, Victorian idea. But over time, and often through the hard knocks of experience, Keynes would move from operating as a speculator to an investor.

Keynes didn't really start speculating or investing in earnest until 1914 (at age 31), according to the editor of his papers, Donald Moggridge.[9]

But his position as bursar at King's College, which he took in 1908 and which involved handling financial accounts and managing the college's investments holdings, would not only deepen his interest in the world of macroeconomics, but it would also give him a first taste of financial markets and the world of speculating on commodities and currency price movements.

Keynes never received a formal introduction or training to financial markets trading and management. At that time, nothing of this sort existed. Most theories were based on esoteric models and even superstition, until Graham formally issued a handbook for professional investment managers in 1934—with Security Analysis co-authored with Frank Dodd. The conventional approach at that time was to rely on gossip, or a network of tipsters. Thus, Keynes was little more than a speculator to begin with.

But what separated him and the ordinary speculators of his time were his enormous intellectual powers and the rigorous academic methodology he applied to studying it. What he learned he would write down and pass on to his group of followers and students. In so doing, he further deepened his understanding of the subject matter.

Using his knowledge of international finance, Keynes took to the currency markets with abandon. "He wanted to make money in a hurry in the 1920s," his biographer Robert Skidelsky declared in an interview, "and thought gambling on currencies (when currencies were floating in the early 1920s) was the way to do it."[10]

With the support of close friends and relatives, Keynes set up an investing syndicate in 1920 which many financial historians claim was one of the first hedge funds. Rather than managing money for the preservation of capital or for yield, Keynes was purely and simply speculating.

At first, his strategy paid off, netting $30,000 for his investors in the first few months. By April 1920, notes Liaquat Ahamed in The Lords of Finance, Keynes had made an additional $80,000, which was astounding considering that most of Europe was essentially financially wrecked from the war.

In a classic case of "beginners luck," his early speculations paid off handsomely. But what was unclear at that time was where his success came from. Even Keynes himself was unsure whether his success was the result of expertise and analysis, or whether he was experiencing a run of luck in the bull markets. He would soon find out.

Then something unexpected happened: "Suddenly, in the space of four weeks, a spasm of optimism about Germany briefly drove the declining European currencies back up, wiping out their entire investment account."[11]

Keynes's doting father, Neville, came to the rescue and bailed out his now middle-aged son with a "birthday present," while Keynes himself secured a loan from the financier Sir Ernest Cassel. From a position of (relatively speaking) destitution, Keynes was back in the game. By the end of 1922, he had $120,000 in his account. That was nearly $1.7 million in today's money.[12]

As is usual with many successful speculators who lose despite their enormous skills, over time, he was right on his currency bets. But he got burned in the short run. In his pitch to Cassel, although Keynes humbly admitted, "I am not in a position to risk any capital myself, having quite exhausted my resources," once again he flashed his confidence. "I anticipate very substantial profits with very good probability if you are prepared to stand the racket for perhaps a couple of months."[13]

Not only did Keynes jump back on the speculation steed, but he was able to repay all of his investors by the end of 1922 and sat on a small profit. Now he turned his sights on an even more volatile market—the commodity markets.

In 1924, Keynes started investing on behalf of King's College, Cambridge, from his position as Bursar. He applied the principles of macroeconomics in his investment strategies, as he was highly knowledgeable in that particular field. This, however, led to a huge run of dismal results that lasted into the early 1930s.

He placed the college's finances into a chest with the intention of increasing the chest value with his tremendous trading and investment skills. The chest was enhanced through the sale of property, but Keynes' policy was opposed by many of the ultra-conservative college fellows. Over time, he convinced even his harshest critics of his enormous investment skills and capability to generate returns for the University, as he transformed himself from a young amateur speculator to one of the most successful investors of his time.

### *Keynes the Investor—From Saulus to Paulus*

Keynes never shied away from taking calculated risks, in his life and as well with his own money. But by definition, risk means also the chance of loss. As Keynes moved into the 1920s and began to invest in commodities, he could not anticipate the world depression. By then he had accumulated net assets totaling more than $3.4 million (in today's money) he had deployed in risk commodities contracts.

But everything in world markets began to change in 1928, and when prices began to drop, he was still long in rubber, wheat, cotton, and tin. By 1930, after Wall Street had crashed and the world had plunged into the Great Depression, wholesale prices had plummeted 20 percent. Many commodities—wheat, cotton, wool, silk, sugar, rubber, and metals—took a 50 percent hit. After the stock market crash of 1929, Keynes eventually lost some 80 percent of his net worth, forcing him to put some of his paintings on the market.

For the second time, Keynes had lost a fortune. Despite his economic knowledge and superior understanding of the markets, the humbling experience of having nearly lost two fortunes changed his thinking on the best way to invest. The macro view of trying to guess where the economy was moving, and to link currency and commodity trades to those hunches, had failed in a big way. His new focus on confidence, sentiment, and psychology made all of his extensive research into prices, supply/demand ratios, and monetary movement seem irrelevant.

He painfully realized that he had to rethink his investment approach and personal risk management. And in one of the most astounding examples of personal improvement and change, Keynes completely overhauled his investment approach from being a modern-day day trader and speculator to becoming an enlightened investor.

After yet more extensive studies of his own mistakes, Keynes believed that to generate success, an investor had to concentrate his investment in enterprises about which he was knowledgeable. To Keynes, this was the end of an investment strategy known as "industrial index," which dominated the era. An investor's knowledge, no matter how widely he may think, is generally limited to about three areas of expertise. According to Keynes, he must therefore commit his investment into these enterprises, hence improving the probability of financial success.

Keynes selected investments with "great care and confidently adhered to what he had chosen through dark days."[14] According to Harrod, Keynes now developed the view that speculation is economically detrimental. He strongly believed that investors are safe when speculating on a predictable enterprise but can be hurt when an enterprise is dependent on speculation. In Keynes words, according to Harrod:

*"Investing is an activity of forecasting the yield over the life of the asset; speculation is the activity of forecasting the psychology of the market."*[15]

But he also knew the uncertainty and unpredictability of financial markets. He understood that these markets just could not be captured by mathematical and forecasting models. Room for interpretation and personal judgement had to always be left. This is most clearly expressed in his famed quote: "I would rather be vaguely right than precisely wrong."

Then, from 1932-1937, the economic world changed once more. Few people realize that this was the second-greatest rally of the twentieth century, after the 1921-1929 boom (which provided as much bust as it did boom). U.S. stocks alone rose nearly 280% during the 1930s rebound. Keynes stayed in the market throughout the decade, although he took some punishing losses from 1937 up until World War II. Then, from 1942-1946, there was another incredibly counterintuitive event. The Germans were bombing London close to submission with the blitz, British ships were being sunk by the score, and matters were looking pretty grim for Europe, at least until D-Day in 1944. Keynes, however, managed to hold on to his portfolio. U.S. stocks rose 122 % during that time. According to the Leuthold Group, he finished strong in his stewardship of his own—and institutional—funds.

As we reach the end of our study of the financial life of John Maynard Keynes, we can draw some conclusions. His financial journey was tempestuous; he was a man who made mistakes; errors of judgement befell him at times; and he was a man never afraid to upset the establishment. He may have lost a fortune—twice—but he made one three times. That is a good return. When he died in 1946, Keynes was a very rich man.

## Winston Churchill: The British Bulldog

*"We make a living by what we get, but we make a life by what we give."—Winston Churchill*

If you have ever visited the small town of Woodstock, to the north of Oxford in England, then the chances are you will have seen Blenheim Palace and its grounds. Not all of them, unless you had a very long time to fill. This emblem of British wealth and might extends to around 2,000 acres, features colonnades, turrets, towers and ballrooms in its main building, while statues and follies grace its ground.

It is the home of Winston Churchill, indomitable British Bulldog; conqueror of the most wicked regime to ever threaten the world—Nazi Germany; Prime Minister; and fearless soldier and author. History's greatest Englishman (in the view of the English, at least). Surely, with such a career, such a home, Winston Churchill epitomizes financial success? Or not.

Was Winston Churchill an impeccable man who overcame stuttering in his childhood and defeated the Nazis?[16] Or a bullish chancer, an outspoken bully who got lucky when it mattered but often failed at what he sought to achieve? The answer, probably, is a bit of both. It is just that defeating Hitler rather skews things in his favor. Naturally, therefore, less attention has been paid to his financial life than his political or military achievements. Considering the immense success that Winston Churchill had in his career as a soldier, writer, war leader and politician, was he effective when making financial decisions in his personal life? As the grandson of a duke, did he inherit fortunes? How did he live? Surrounded by manservants and housemaids? Brought up largely by a nanny (then again, he was a bit of a disappointment to his father, Randolph, himself a successful politician, but one who died young, probably from syphilis. Meanwhile, his mother was generally busy in her "social" life, one which was certainly extremely social).

## *Churchill's Formative Years*

Young Winston Churchill was born into aristocracy; his father was the Duke of Marlborough. He was also a firebrand politician, womanizer and bully; his mother, Jennie Jerome, was an American socialite.

Winston was never a good student. A rebellious streak lived in him, something not tolerated in the realm of the British public school system. Following beatings and obstinance, he changed his boarding prep school (a type of school for the wealthy elite of British society, catering to children—boys in those days—up to the age of 13. It is highly ironic that the "public" schools were anything but public). At one boarding school, as was the custom on Parents' Day, the students were marching in in academic order—Winston was last—to the full amusement to the other parents whom all knew his father, Lord Randolph. One of his tutors complained, that, though acknowledging Winston's raw intellect, bitterly complained about his lack of discipline, his irregularity, his desire to learn only the things he wanted to learn. The tutor concluded that these would pose an insurmountable barrier to his future career—if he could find any. Clearly a fine judge of character.

In particular, learning Latin or Greek was a menace to Winston—later he would be proud of his resistance to traditional schooling and the studies of the classic. "No one ever made me write a Latin verse, and I never learned Greek beyond the alphabet!" he said in his characteristic growl.

Churchill's father was an Eton man. Unusual for a boy with an aristocratic background, the Berkshire hive of privilege turned him down, and he was forced to attend Harrow instead. This was, in those days, considered home to the rich, but less talented and without the promising future of an accomplished political career. It was a failure to which Randolph would often refer.

Although generally school was a chore, there was one subject in which he excelled. That was English. He also displayed a love for history—military history in particular. From Harrow, he was considered clever enough only to enter a military academy, rather than a University (another cause for criticism from his father) and joined the exclusive home to Officers in the making, Sandhurst.

So began a distinguished military career that would bring forward a different side of his character. It was during the early days of this military career that his nanny, whom he called Woomany, died. Once Winston had been sent off to school, Woomany had been dismissed from service. It is a sign of Winston's softer side that he financed the remainder of her life and made sure that could visit her on her deathbed and arrange for her funeral.

Like many ambitious young men of his time, he wanted to see military action, and his wish would be granted. Wounded, captured and eyewitness to the consequences of modern warfare, Churchill developed additional character traits of fortitude and strength of mind that would serve him throughout his political life.

It would also bring out another trait that would follow him throughout his life—in good as well as bad times—Churchill the gambler. Churchill's calculations and decision-making were decided mostly on gut instinct rather than evidence or common sense; even sometimes self-preservation. On one well-documented occasion, serving in Africa, he rode up and down in front of enemy guns, while the opposition shot at him. On another, he led a cavalry charge that should, by all standards, have resulted in the slaughter of himself and his men. The impetuosity of the act seemed to subdue the enemy into subservience, and the charge was successful.

But it was when stationed in India, that he found his true passion: reading. Being fed by his mother one book after another, Winston enjoyed reading certain types of books rather than seeking those works that were popular at his time. It is said that he simply focused on a few great novels he would read over and over again, even committing many to memory—a skill that would serve him well later in Parliament, and especially during his great speeches of the war years.

Despite the apparent spontaneity of these, they were in fact carefully prepared and learned by rote. The book that most likely influenced him the most was Edward Gibbon's The Rise and Fall of The Roman Empire. Gibbon's powerful prose can be found echoed in Churchill's own writings. It was during these formative years as a young cadet, full of dreams and hope and eager for military adventure, that he really developed his style of writing—the powerful English prose for which Churchill today is so famous. It would serve him well financially, as well as securing his place in literary history.

### Churchill's Work and Income

As a young army officer, he saw action in British India, the Anglo-Sudan War, and the Second Boer War. He gained fame as a war correspondent and wrote books about his campaigns, which made him an instant darling with the British press at home and he gained a way to earn money for himself, besides gaining a large crowd of followers—which would later prepare him for his political career.

His first noteworthy writing assignment was when he was dispatched on his first military campaign. His mother ensured that he received payments that were the equivalent of $130,000 in today's valuation for his journalism.[17]

Clark reported that after Churchill won the seat of Oldham at the 1900 general election (it was inevitable, really, that he would follow his father into politics), he immediately went on a speaking tour throughout the United States and Britain, raising £10,000 for himself (about $1,300,000 today's valuation).[18]

He would remain in Parliament for most of the remainder of his life until his retirement, at the age of 88, after the 1964 General Election.

After a short break, following deselection for his constituency, he returned to government under the Prime Minister, Lloyd George.

At the outbreak of the Second World War, he was again appointed First Lord of the Admiralty. Following the resignation of Neville Chamberlain on May 10, 1940, Churchill became Prime Minister. He led Britain as Prime Minister until after the German surrender in 1945. His defeat at the first general election to take place after the conflict remains one of the greatest shocks in not only British, but global, political history.

Following the war, he raised concerns about growing Communist rule in Eastern Europe, coining the phrase "Iron Curtain" regarding the growth of Soviet influence in Europe.

### Churchill's Home Budgeting and Spending Habits

Churchill has been the subject of many biographers. One who took a closer look at the private financial life of Winston Churchill was David Lough, who examined both his income sources and his spending habits.

Most people assumed Churchill was rich due to his aristocratic background and his flagrant lifestyle. However, he was not born into a family of great wealth and he did not marry into a great fortune (most of Churchill's money coming from his American mother's side). Although Churchill's family loved to talk of him marrying an heiress, when he finally walked the aisle at the age of 33, he married Clementine for love. Clementine had a poor background, even though her father was a successful businessman. Unfortunately, he left home while Clementine was still young, and rarely offered them any financial support. Hence, prior to the marriage, Clementine worked as a seamstress and taught French to make ends meet.[19] Churchill took his time before proposing to his future wife, and when he did, it was from the bench with the best view in the whole of Blenheim Palace—an impressive sight indeed.

In 1921, his cousin and benefactor died, and Winston Churchill inherited a valuable estate in Wales.[20] But his financial comfort wouldn't last, as we shall see later. He lived on his Chartwell estate, but in 1946, he complained to Lord Camrole, a good friend of his, that he had money problems. Missing out on his lucrative income as Prime Minister, he felt that he might have to leave Parliament altogether and focus on full-time writing. He even considered selling his beloved home at Chartwell. Lord Camrole was horrified that Britain's War Leader and National Hero should find himself in such dire straits. He offered a substantial sum to the former leader for the estate, which he then leased back at a peppercorn rate, the home reverting to the National Trust (a British trust which maintains stately homes for the nation) on his death.

Churchill may have been a political giant of his generation, yet his personal financial operations were less than stellar, especially when compared to Keynes. Much is written about Churchill's legacy, but let us here focus on the financial aspects of his life.

Research by D. Lough has found that Churchill was reckless with the spending of his income.[21]

In spite of the money he gained through his writing career, which would have been enough to make most writers wealthy today—never mind Churchill's own era—his love for drinks and good foods, luxuries, gambling and reckless spending, which he inherited from his parents, made him live on the financial cliff edge for most of his life. Indeed, as an old man, suffering deafness and increasingly regular strokes, he would still live the high life on the French Riviera.

Winston Churchill's annual expenses were about £40,000 (which is about $1.3 million in today's valuation). A great amount of his expenditure was on a staff of footmen and Swiss nurses (all vetted by MI5, although given the past record of that organization, this probably counted for little). He won £12,000 ($390,000 in today's money) as the winner of the Nobel Prize for Literature. Lough reported that Winston Churchill ordered in 1908, the year that he got married to Clementine, the following items: 72 bottles of whisky, 108 bottles of Pol Roger 1895 vintage champagne, 60 bottles of St Estephe (red) wine, 84 bottles of sparkling Moselle (white) wine, 36 bottles of 20-year-old brandy, 4 bottles of gin and 26 bottles of vermouth. During the darkest days of World War II, ensconced deep underground in his bunker from where he ran the war campaign, he still functioned best after copious quantities of the best brandy and several of the large cigars for which he is famous.[22]

Considering the enormous amount of alcohol that Winston Churchill ordered and consumed annually, it is clear that he needed vast wealth to fund his lifestyle. Fortunately, he had an understanding wine merchant in Randolph Payne and Sons.[23] They had been the official wine merchant of the Churchill family for generations. However, when his outstanding balance grew to $75,000 in today's valuation, the chairman had to write him. This led to one of Churchill's financial measures. Most notably is the "No more Champagne."

It is not quite proven whether Churchill made use of financial experts, of which there were many in the City of London (the modern day equivalent of Wall Street and financial center of the British Empire). His regular and confidential meetings with the head of the Internal Revenue Board, in which he discussed his tax situation, would be considered highly inappropriate and probably illegal today. Churchill developed many enemies during his life, but few were disliked as much as the taxman, one of his few opponents he never quite managed to defeat. Rich friends such as Sir Ernest Cassel and Sir Henry Strakosch bailed him out of his debts and taxes and at one point, the government had to settle his bills.[24]

## *Churchill the Gambler and Speculator*

What made his spending habit worse (with the resulting tendency to fall into debt) was his peculiar relationship with gambling and risk taking. Churchill had a routinely unlucky losing streak in Monte Carlo in Monaco. In an excellent essay written for The Telegraph, Nicholas Shakespeare said that Clementine Churchill, on more than one occasion, admonished her husband to "beware the Casino." And while it was increasingly the case that speculators of Churchill's financial weight would employ advisers to at least offer some expertise behind their gambles, in stocks (as in other aspects of his life), Churchill felt he knew best. "I have managed several clients in my career and I have never encountered anybody who took risks on such a high scale" one of his early financial advisors recounted.[25]

Winston Churchill left bills, bank statements, tax demands and investment records in his archive that showed evidence of his profligate gambling and debts. In the documents, there were phases where he traded shares, currencies and gambled with an intensity that seemed to be devoid of restraint, while he brimmed with energy and self-confidence. "It excited me so much to play like a foolish moth," Churchill explained.[26]

The biggest blow to Churchill's fortune came with the big crash in 1929. In the fateful year of 1929, he was traveling across the United States with his son when he wrote to his wife Clementine, with the confidence of a novice trader:

> *"How wonderful financial security is. My stocks are just booming in America and now that I am out of office I can write, but I can write the kind of things I want to, without worrying about writing for a living."*[27]

We all know what happened in October 1929. Shakespeare revealed that Churchill lost over $12 million in today's valuation when the stock market crashed in 1929. A hefty sum for anybody, and hardly inspiring of confidence in someone who held public office.

According to Lough, Churchill had brokers who advised him via telegraph and telephone. However, being a high-risk taker, he often ignored their advice. On one particular occasion, Churchill bought and sold shares worth £420,000 at the time (which is more than $5 million at today's valuation). His brokers warned him by telegraph: "Market heavy. Liquidating becoming more urgent. Will await your telephone. Your bank still losing gold and there are rumors of increase in bank rate."[28]

Of course, he wasn't alone in losing a fortune in this historic stock market crash. Like many other punters, he wasn't able to back up this position when the recovery finally came almost a decade later. But all was not lost.

His wife, Clementine, sighed with relief when she found that Churchill had inherited the valuable estate in Wales between the war years. She felt "that we need never, never be worried about money again." Winston Churchill would spend the inherited fortune in heavy serial gambling—in the casino as well as in stocks—to the horror of his wife.[29]

What always brought him out of his self-inflicted financial misery was his writing. He would publish a series of national and global masterpieces that would keep his financial head above the pecuniary seas of bankruptcy. And he was a popular speaker right up until his death. Winston Churchill was a man always able to make money, but one who found it very hard to keep.

## Comparing John Maynard Keynes with Winston Churchill

Frederick Leith-Ross, chief economic adviser to the UK government from 1932 to 1945, described both Churchill and Keynes as prominent, clever, opinionated and combative, which inevitably attracted criticism. In the heat of debate, Churchill and Keynes could be disparaging about each other. During the 1929 election campaign, Churchill referred to "Professor Keynes" as "the proprietor or controller of an extreme radical weekly newspaper," while Keynes declared a statement by Churchill to be "feather-brained."[30] It is probably not unsurprising that the two held little respect for the views of the other. There is Keynes—analytical, mathematical, even calculating the impact of gut instinct. On the other side is Winston Churchill—gambler, big thinker, doer at whatever cost.

But for all of this, through most of their public lives, they frequently expressed mutual regard. Keynes "had not only an intellectual appreciation" of Churchill's gifts, but a "warmth of sympathy for one whose type of mind was very different from his own."

Time magazine included Keynes among its Most Important People of the Century in 1999; The Economist has described Keynes as "Britain's most famous 20th-century economist."[31] Yet, they couldn't be more different. And that means each offer differing but valuable financial lessons from which we can learn. Let's look at what united them and what made those giants of history so different.

Churchill was short and overweight, but lived to an old age; Keynes was tall and gangly, but fragile in his health and would die much too soon. While they were physically and emotionally poles apart, they could be considered the two greatest Britons of the 20th century—and if not, each of them certainly sits at the top table. Bertrand Russell called Maynard Keynes "the sharpest and clearest intellect that I have ever known." Late history professor Rufus Fears called Winston Churchill the "greatest statesman who ever lived." Maynard Keynes was an academic intellectual, Churchill a military adventurist. Neither figure was without controversy, and each incurred harsh criticism in their time and even today. History's perspective changes with time, and as we remember the war years through the increasingly few survivors of that conflict, so Winston Churchill seems to grow in stature, if such a situation was possible.

And while Keynesian economics fell out of favor for a short while around the late 1990s and early 2000s, the world recession instigated in the main by the sub-prime crisis demonstrated that governments cannot leave economics to control itself; intervention is sometimes needed.

Born in 1874 and 1883, respectively, they were near contemporaries: Churchill the aristocrat and politician, Keynes the middle-class intellectual. Both lived at a crucial time in world history, economically and politically. If Churchill's background was more aristocratic, Keynes' was more socially aware. If Churchill learned to oppose the worst excesses of British rule, such as the Amritsar Massacre in India of 1919, then Keynes took lessons from the financial and economic gains Britain extracted from its Empire, notwithstanding any moral rights or wrongs.

Churchill, the aristocrat, with a mother from a rich but barely acceptable American background; Keynes with a mother who ticked all the right social boxes, but in terms of money, was comparatively poor.

Keynes the intellectual; Churchill with an instinctive wit. Keynes from, according to the economist and biographer Robert Skidelsky, a loving, caring home; Churchill brought up by a nanny and with parents to whom he always felt he was either a slight hindrance or a considerable disappointment.

Perhaps it was these differences that led the two to adopt such radically different approaches to their financial lives. Churchill always looking for the big win, for the achievement that would make him, according to politician and biographer Boris Johnson, acceptable in the eyes of his father. Keynes more confident, with the sort of secure background that allowed him to be analytical—cold even—with his economic calculations.

But for all the differences, they shared great similarities in their lives as well. Both came from relatively privileged backgrounds; each attended the most socially exclusive schools of their day. Both were great writers and used their writing as early sources of income. Neither started life with a lot of ready cash, so to speak, and earned their fortunes through their endeavors. Both, at times, saw their financial worth disappear. Keynes largely got his back through his intellect and wit; Churchill through native cunning and links to the corridors of power. In that sense, each possessed the frailties we all hold, but also had access to advantages that apply to few of us.

When it comes to financial comparisons, Keynes, the economist, come out as the clear winner over Churchill, the politician. Churchill was a notorious spender and gambler; Keynes was in control of his spending, speculations and investments.

While Churchill's personal finances dwindled with the fall in the general British stock market and later a complete wipe out in the great crash of 1929, Keynes's fund grew at an annual compounding rate of 9.1 percent for the rest of his life. The gambler's outcome against the revenues of the analyst. The lesson is clear.

According to Harrod, Keynes selected investments with great care and boldly adhered to what he had chosen even through periods of adverse market developments, while Winston Churchill made investment decisions based on his instinct at any given time. That instinct often depended on his mood and, unsurprisingly perhaps given his upbringing, Churchill was a near-depressive.

Both had the potential to be financially successful, not least through their skills as writers, collectors of fine art, oratorical talents and roles within Government. It is just that there were far many more ups and downs in the ride of Churchill's financial roller coaster when compared to that of Keynes.

Two great men. Two pioneers. Two men from whom we can draw valuable financial lessons. And so on to two more examples of the rich and famous as we move away from the rather mundane field of politics and academia to the glamour world of Hollywood and movie fame.

## Chapter 2
# STARS FROM HOLLYWOOD

In the shimmering world of the rich and famous, no other aspect of society is more glamorous than the lives of the movie stars of Hollywood. Fame and fortune often make us think of the usual celebrity lifestyle that goes hand-in-hand with any big name in Hollywood: An endless flow of cash, million-dollar bank accounts, extravagance, excess, prime real estate, and luxury cars. Drugs and plenty of affairs often feature as well.

Controversy seems to follow Hollywood stars wherever they go. Take, for example, Tom Cruise, multi-million-dollar actor, creative talent and, judging from the chat shows and comments of others, thoroughly great guy. But mention his name, and the first thought that comes to most people's minds is his relationship with scientology, a misunderstood belief system if ever there was one. Or the ongoing and—let's be honest—somewhat boring Brangelina debacle.

It has always been so. Hollywood greats from yesteryear, such as Marilyn Monroe, were the subject of gossip and scandal—even when these were based on nothing more than hearsay. The lives of Elizabeth Taylor and Richard Burton were a catalogue of marriages and divorces. They wed each other just twice.

Even so, when it comes to making—and more importantly keeping—their wealth, the stars of Hollywood have much from which we can learn.

## *Jennifer Lawrence—The Upstanding Kentucky Girl*

*"Even as far back as when I started acting at 14, I know I've never considered failure."—Jennifer Lawrence*

Of course, not every star and starlet out there lives up (or down, however you look at it) to this stereotype. In fact, many well-known A-listers are actually some of the most financially astute people—maybe even more so than non-celebrities.

One star who is continually pointed to as a perfect example of a financially responsible person is Jennifer Lawrence. It's hard to open a newspaper or click on a news site without seeing her name. This isn't all that surprising, considering that she, an Oscar winner, has recently been named as the highest-earning actress in the world for the second year running.

According to sources, her net worth was estimated to be $130 million in 2017.[32] That's not bad for a lady from Kentucky who constantly has to deal with the limelight that comes from being a star of Hollywood and who, despite this, manages to stay out of private and financial trouble.

### *Lawrence's Upbringing and Career*

Jennifer Shrader Lawrence was born in 1990 in Louisville, Kentucky, in a comfortable, though humble, middle-class family.

She lived with her parents and two older brothers on a farm on the outskirts of town. They were raised in an extremely stable background and were taught the importance of traditional family values and the spirit of community. Karen and Gary Lawrence were engaging parents who also engrained the value of making sound financial management decisions in all their children right from a young age.

Lawrence was spotted at the age of 14 by the CESD Talent

Agency in Union Square. She had traveled with her family to New York for the spring vacation. This acted as a launching pad to an illustrious career as an actress in the entertainment world. But keeping their daughter's feet on the ground was always a priority for the Lawrence parents. They had an agreement with the agency for her to complete the remaining part of her high school before they would let her focus solely on an acting career. This proved a great motivation for her, as she went on to graduate from high school in a record two years before her time. [33]

She got her major breakthrough in the entertainment scene in 2006 when she performed in the television program Company Town. This also gave her an opportunity to play various roles in several comedy shows. After performing as a 17-year-old in Winter Bone, Jennifer went on to be nominated for an Academy Award Oscar for the Best Actress role. Even though she did not win that award, she earned enormous acclaim for her nomination—it was the year 2011 and Jennifer was just 20 years of age, making her one of the youngest nominees in the history of the Oscars. [34]

Her performance in the 2013 film Silver Linings Playbook, together with Bradley Cooper and Robert De Niro, earned her both an Academy Award and a Golden Globe Award for Best Actress. For her 2013 role in American Hustle, she went on to win a Golden Globe for Best Supporting Actress and a third nomination for an Academy Award. [35]

With all the international praise and industry accolades, the money started rolling in early on.

The various roles she has played have not only earned her praise, but also a number of good paychecks. The Burning Plain (2009) earned her $20,000; Winter Bone (2010) earned her an average of $3,000 a week; The Beaver (2011) raked in $80,000 for her and X-Men: First Class (2011) earned her $250,000. The Hunger Games (2011) saw her draw her first million-dollar fee. Her Oscar winning performance in Silver Linings Playbook (2012) earned her $400,000 (it was a much smaller budget film than The Hunger Games) and The Hunger Games: Mockingjay - Part 1 (2014) saw her move into the serious big-time with a whopping $15,000,000 fee.

In 2016, she is reported to have earned about $46 million, which included her salary from Passenger ($20 million). In 2017, she earned $24 million and in 2018 (at the time of this writing), she has earned $15 million so far for her role as Dominika Egorova in

The Red Sparrow.[36]

In addition to the film-related revenue, the annual Forbes List from which the information above has been extracted also takes earnings from product endorsements and sponsorship deals into account, such as her advertising campaigns for the Dior fashion house, for which she works as a "brand ambassador."

### *Spending Habits*

When it comes to spending and handling her accumulated wealth, she is officially represented by the management group Creative Artists Agency (CAA) through Alexandra Trustman and Jeremy Plager. Yet, the success and prudence of handling her money can be traced back to Lawrence herself. In Hollywood, she's known for sticking to the lessons of her childhood and being frugal.[37]

Her financial management basis springs back to where she was born and brought up. It is from this setting that she acquired appropriate know-how on the way she should conduct herself. "J. Law," as she is fondly known, credits her mother, a camp counselor, and her father, a former construction firm owner, for instilling in her good financial values from the start.

Although they were not poor, money was limited for the Lawrence family when their daughter was growing up. Therefore, her parents had to really show their kids the importance of budgets and, in essence, the skill of prioritizing what they needed.

Her mother, Karen Lawrence, being a staunch Christian, wanted her children to be brought up with strong morals and sincerely-held values. It is even reported that at the time when Jennifer Lawrence wanted to go into mainstream acting, she prayed for her to fail, worried that the world of Hollywood might adversely influence her daughter. Nothing could, of course, be further than the truth. Her attitude, she asserted, changed when her daughter made them proud by sticking to her values and adhering to the morals she was brought up with. Of course, at the same time, she was also succeeding big time with her venture into acting.

The other outstanding factor in Jennifer Lawrence's family that has given her a level head, even after having such a huge windfall from her acting career, is the fact that their family is very close-knit. This ensures that whenever any one of them sees the other behaving in a manner which is contrary to their upbringing, other family members are on hand to bring them back in line. This is a very strong basis for common sense decisions.

"I was raised to have value for money, to have respect for money, even though you have a lot of it," Jennifer told the U.K. magazine Fabulous last year. "My family is not the kind of family that would ever let me turn into an a**hole or anything like that, so I am fortunate to have them." What kinds of frugal banking habits does Lawrence practice? For one, she still lives modestly for a celebrity in Los Angeles. Lawrence has no personal assistants to do her shopping, and she won't be found frequenting any uber-high-scale stores, preferring to clip coupons. She's also reluctant to use valet parking. Indeed, she eschews the drop-dead Jaguars and Bentleys, Porsches and Cadillacs typically found in the multi-car garages of other Hollywood superstars, instead for many years driving the same Volkswagen she's owned since before fame made her rich. Since her Best Actress win for Silver Linings Playbook, however, she has been spotted in a new Chevy Volt, bought at a whopping $39,000 price tag!

Jennifer also said that she couldn't envision spending lots of money on frivolous purchases. Frugality is ingrained in her lifestyle. Combined with her smart financial choices, Jennifer is one of Hollywood's rare figures, commanding high earnings through pure talent—and using them to good measure. She chooses to spend only enough to get by.[38]

Jennifer Lawrence is a member of a new generation of financially literate celebrities (like Zooey Deschanel or Ashton Kutcher) who make smart financial choices.

As a model in financial management, Jennifer Lawrence is virtually unique within her peer group. Her financial muscle makes her revered even among the mighty egos of Hollywood.

## *Investing Her Money*

J ennifer Lawrence breaks the mold of how many Hollywood A-list celebrities conduct their financial business. Her down-to-earth personality might seem in direct opposition to the vast sums she earns as the industry's highest-paid actress. Indeed, given some of her spending, people might even conclude that money is tight for her. Again, this myth is a reflection of her sensible upbringing.

Like many Hollywood celebrities, Jennifer Lawrence eventually went on to buy a mansion for herself in Beverly Hills, California.

This house was initially owned by Ellen DeGeneres and TV star Jessica Simpson. The total cost of this particular home was $7 million. Previously, she had sold her condominium for $1.15 million, raking in a sizeable profit ($271,000) for a house she acquired initially for just $879,000. There is limited information on Jennifer Lawrence's investment portfolio, as most of her investment decisions are handled by her agents in CAA. Nevertheless, her business in real estate is typical of her considered approach.

### *Fighting for Her Rights*

Jennifer has always been prepared to stand up for what is right, and that included her financial compensation. She has previously spoken out about the gender pay gap in Hollywood, pointing out in a 2015 essay that actresses are still often paid less than their male counterparts. This controversy rocked when Jennifer Lawrence confirmed that in the year 2015, she made less than her male colleagues. The megastar made headlines with her essay "Why Do I Make Less Than My Co-stars?" describing "the lucky people with dicks" who are paid much more than their female counterparts. Jennifer worked for 19 days and was paid $1.25 million, for her work on American Hustle. In addition to this, she received $250,000 in deferred compensation. She was also given seven points in profit participation.

Meanwhile, Christian Bale (a male counterpart) worked 45 days for $2.5 million up-front and nine points, while Bradley Cooper worked 46 days for $2.5 million and nine points. These differing payment amounts are what inspired Jennifer to speak up through Lenny Letter, a feminist online newsletter owned by Lena Dunham, on October 13, 2015.[39]

Evidently, her words made an impact. In her new film, Passengers, although her screen time is decidedly less than her co-star Chris Pratt, her salary was $20 million versus his $12 million. Her financial success continued, driven by her ever-greater earning potential.

### *Family, a Source of Strength*

Undoubtedly, a part of that ability to retain privacy comes from her (apparently) faultless personal life. Even though Jennifer Lawrence has had a fair share of relationships, this has not resulted in either scandal or financial losses through divorce.

However, her romantic life has been fulfilling. From dating a rock star, an actor and now a director, this leading lady has had a wide-range of real-life love interests, but has not allowed these to interfere with either her career or her finances. If the past is any guidance, it's unlikely that such an event will ever happen, whomever she finally chooses as a permanent life partner.[40]

Given the above, it is no surprise that Jennifer Lawrence is a role model and an idol to young people. She possesses unique qualities, which make her a perfect fit for the modern world.

Her family exemplifies a supportive but moderating influence on children. They will not just sit back and wait to see their humble daughter follow the river and drown. Once more, she re-writes the Hollywood script of the prima donna movie star—the diva who demands, and gets, whatever she wants.

Her parents and brothers are very supportive of her; they know her well and want the best for her. This is another very important aspect of investing; the need to surround ourselves with people who want to see us grow, flourish and utilize our maximum potential. Jennifer, therefore, seems headed in the right direction to avoid the traditional pitfalls of stardom. With constant guidance from those around her, she uses that advice to her best advantage.

She remains charming and vivacious, socially as well as financially.

## *Johnny Depp—The Eccentric Pirate*

*"You use your money to buy privacy because during most of your life, you aren't allowed to be normal." —Johnny Depp*

Most things in life have a good side…and a bad one, dark parts and bright parts. There are two sides to every coin. For every Jennifer Lawrence, there is a Johnny Depp. In fact, several of them.

The Jack Sparrow actor is perhaps best known for his outstanding performances in the Pirates of The Caribbean movies. These have earned him fame, wealth and the ear of the most powerful people in Hollywood.

While, over the years, Depp has made a lot of money from his various starring film roles, he has never really learned how to manage it. He is almost the caricature of the Hollywood A-list actor. His star shines so brightly: his talent is enormous, his income almost beyond comprehension. Yet at the same time, his lifestyle is like his fashion quirks—a constant drama.

For all that, Johnny Depp can offer us lessons to learn, and like him, they are entertaining in the extreme.

### *Upbringing and Career*

Depp was born John Christopher Depp in Owensboro, Kentucky, in 1963 to John and Betty Sue Depp. He is the youngest among four children. His father was a civil engineer, and his mother was a waitress and a housewife. He admitted that as a child he was introverted, and his parents even thought he had Tourette's syndrome. Johnny says that they rarely settled in any place for long because they had to accommodate his father's work commitments. They eventually arrived in Miramar, Florida, when Depp was just 7 years old. They rented a hotel room until his father gained a job. Depp abhorred his new home. By just 12 years of age, he says that he had begun to experiment with drugs. The reason for this was to release the stresses that came from his family's problems.

Three years later, when Johnny was 15 years, his parents separated. Although relationships between him and his father were not good, he would visit his father for a weekly trial so that his mother could get her child support. Eventually, Johnny severed ties with his father altogether.

When Depp was 16 years old, he dropped out of school and established a garage band, The Kids. They became so popular that they opened for the "Talking Heads" and the "B-52s."

At 20 years of age, Johnny met up with make-up artist, Lori Allison, five years his senior, and they got married the same year, in 1983. The newlyweds quickly moved to Los Angeles in the hopes of a breakthrough for Depp's band. Like many who traveled west, only to see their dreams smashed, the group failed to make it big. The band found themselves on a very tight budget, which they financed through selling pens for a telemarketing entity.

The following year, Lori introduced him to Nicholas Cage, who was her former husband. Through his contacts, Cage introduced the enthusiastic musician to a Hollywood agent, and Depp switched from music into acting. Later on, after Depp had played several parts as an extra or in small roles, he got his first proper breakthrough, appearing in Nightmare in Elm Street, a horror movie made in 1984.

But if his professional life was gaining velocity, Depp's private one was not. His marriage to Lori Allison ended, and through the 1980s he found himself going from one short-term relationship to another.

With his private life up and down, Depp put most of his efforts into studying acting. With a special coach at Loft Studios, he topped his classes. His commitment to studying the profession paid off in 1987 when he succeeded the actor Jeff Yagher in the portrayal of a covert policeman, Tommy Hanson, in the well-known Canadian TV series, 21 Jump Street. This act exposed Depp to practically instant acclaim. He was labeled a teen idol—a title he really abhorred. When his contract with Jump Street ended in

1989, he sought to cast off the teen heartthrob label and chose instead to pursue even more challenging goals.[41]

## *Progression to Money and Fame*

In 1990, Depp built on his career break, starring in Cry Baby, directed by John Walters. In that very same year, he played the eponymous leading role in the Tim Burton fantasy film, Edward Scissorhands. This movie earned $54 million at the box office, gained critical admiration, cult status and, in the process, established Depp as a top-level actor.

In 1994, he re-united with Director Tim Burton on Ed Wood, a biography of the infamously untalented B-movie director. This film went on to earn Depp a particular commendation and another Golden Globe nomination. Other notable films in the late 1990s include Don Juan DeMarco (1995), in which Depp plays a character who believes he is the famous fictional character Don Juan, and Donnie Brasco (1997), which featured Depp as an undercover FBI agent seeking to infiltrate the Bonanno crime family. In 1998, Depp took up the role of journalist Hunter S. Thompson's alter ego in Terry Gilliam's adaptation of Fear and Loathing in Las Vegas. During filming, Depp cultivated a strong friendship with Thompson, which lasted until Thompson's death in 2005. Depp financed his friend's funeral, bringing it to wide public attention (more on this later). He also teamed up with Burton once more in his adaptation of Washington Irvine's Sleepy Hollow, starring as the prim, compulsively driven Ichabod Crane.

In 2004, Depp starred as Jack Sparrow for the first time in the Pirates of the Caribbean. This family adventure movie went on to break box office records and, not least thanks to Depp's critically acclaimed starring role in the movie, the "Pirates" franchise was born. There really had never been a pirate quite like Johnny Depp before. At the close of that year, Depp also turned in a highly-praised performance in Finding Neverland, in which he starred as the Peter Pan creator, J.M. Barrie. The film went on to get him more than 10 award nominations, including both Academy and Golden Globe acknowledgements. Both would contribute greatly to his financial success and still provide him with a substantial and regular income. His career and his finances were well-established.

## *Major Income and Other Earnings*

Most of Depp's earnings were from acting in various movies. In the 26 films in which he has played significant roles, the total box office takings stand at an astonishing $7,800,000,000. His biggest earnings so far have come from the Pirates of the Caribbean franchise. He raked in a total of $85 million from this franchise alone, making him the highest paid actor in 2015. Subsequently, in that year, Forbes named him the "best overpaid actor." There are many who would suggest Depp's unique talents mean he is anything but underpaid.[42]

Depp's production company, Infinitum Nihil, a company he formed in 2004, was, in 2007, rumored to have produced a film about a nationalized former Russian security agent, Alexander Litvinenko, who was poisoned with polonium and murdered in London. The event remains an international mystery, and Depp's involvement in creating a screenplay of the event is one of possibly three to be touted around Hollywood.

## *Peculiar Spending Habits*

More money than he knew how to handle, more problems that he could cope with, and all the typical stereotypes of a Hollywood star. Depp seems to be a typical product of a global game. In the end, due to his minimal financial management education, much of his money has been consumed by his extravagant lifestyle.

Johnny Depp is a man who likes the good life. He is a connoisseur of the finest red wines. He has spent $75 million in acquiring residences all around the world. These include a chateau in France... and an entire island in the Bahamas. He has also built and furnished five luxurious homes in uptown Los Angeles.

He spent $10 million a year to support an entourage of friends, family and personal employees. Also, through the friendship he cultivated with Hunter J. Thompson, he was able to fulfill Thompson's dying wish for his remains to be blasted into the air from a tailor-made cannon over Aspen, Colorado—an event which Depp financed. Depp is also reported to have spent $300,000 on maintaining a staff of 40 full-time employees to keep his houses habitable in case he wanted to use them at short notice.

He also enjoys a fine taste for expensive world-class jewelry, with which he often adorns his flamboyant attire. Depp also had a large assortment of Hollywood collectibles and memorabilia, which involved such megastars as Marilyn Monroe, John Dillinger and Marlon Brando. The collection required 12 storage facilities and millions of dollars to archive.

He also had a reported collection of 45 top-of-the-range cars. His collection of 70 classic guitars runs alongside an extremely expensive art collection, including over 200 collectible pieces and works by world famous artists such as Warhol, Klimt, Basquiat, and Modigliani. It was also reported that he spent $18 million on his 150-foot long yacht in the Bahamas.[43]

Depp ended up spending close to $150,000 a month on security guards for himself and his family.

Thus, this very extravagant lifestyle cost, reportedly, $2 million a month. A figure that was not sustainable in the long run.

Johnny Depp is a man obsessed with having a good life. Many family members and associates have tried to dissuade Depp from his opulent lifestyle, but to no avail. The problem for Depp was he got used to his spending habits and, like a drug addict, needed a wake-up call. It arrived, but not one he could have possibly envisioned for himself.

### *Marriage and Divorce*

Depp made one very big financial (if not romantic) mistake when he failed to draft a prenuptial agreement with his now-divorced wife, Amber Heard. Had he done so, it would have made it easier to share the spoils from their marriage amicably rather than seeing his fate hanging on the balance of justice.

He ended up paying his ex-wife $7 million for their separation. This also shows the value of having a close-knit and stable family, people you were brought up with and who supported you morally and socially. Maybe, if he had possessed that same family support as Jennifer Lawrence enjoys, he might have avoided the situation.

After having been married for just 15 months, Amber filed for divorce. With no prenuptial agreement, Depp faced parting with half of the $14 million earnings he amassed while with her, in what turned into a highly-volatile divorce settlement case. Depp followed Amber's directive and donated that amount of money to charity, which he equally apportioned to the American Civil Liberties Union and the Children's Hospital in Los Angeles. He also lost close to $1 million in lawyers' charges through payments to his divorce attorney Laura Wasser.[44]

## *Money Management and being Managed*

From 1999, and spanning 16 years, Johnny Depp's private wealth was managed by The Mandel Group (TMG), which was founded by two attorneys, Joel and Robert Mandel. Depp also had an agent working for him, Tracey Jacobs, who was an employee at UTA. That particular partnership has endured for three decades.

Unfortunately, there was also no binding contract between the management agency and Depp, which was a bad financial management strategy. The management agency, TMG, on several occasions, had tried to advise Mr. Depp regarding his frivolous spending, suggesting that he deviate from this, but they were not in a position to force him into making financial decisions.

After this failed attempt, they incorporated his personal lawyer Jake Bloom, and personal manager Elisa Christie Dembrowski (who is also his sister) to try to mediate on their behalf to help him manage his finances. They suggested he sell off excess properties he owned in order to pay taxes, settle various debts, and enable him to cater for his daily outgoings. This failed too. Depp continued his extravagant spending behavior.

By this point, Depp had already lost touch with his personal finances, preferring to always get advice from his agent, accountant and others who often had an inappropriate investment approach. In the end, he was cheated by his advisors, many of whom also charged him exorbitant fees.

They collected $28 million in contingency fees that Depp says he never agreed to. They exploited Depp's tendency to avoid written contracts and rely on verbal agreements, which allowed them to create doubt in what had been arranged.

Depp also lost considerable sums through his management team's actions. They failed to ensure that his financial excesses were well-managed and kept at bay. They needed to ensure that they did not hurt his image. They owed him a duty in the contract to ensure that his excessive spending came to an end—however, it did not.

In the event that Depp disregarded their advice, the Management Group might have had an obligation to cut ties with the actor, or at the very least, stop paying itself millions of dollars from his accounts. They failed to honor this responsibility—

morally, if not legally—even when they apparently saw that Depp was grinding himself towards financial ruin.

Depp claimed that TMG consistently failed to file or pay his taxes on time, costing him $5.6 million in federal penalties and interest; he claimed they had also failed to keep proper books and loaned nearly $10 million of his money to third parties without authorization. He also confirmed that TMG was self-dealing by investing his money in business ventures in which they had ownership interests.

In March 2016, upon realizing that he was paying a high commission to his sister, Elisa, as a personal manager, he opted out and signed a contract with her rival company, CAA. This move took place later on in October 2016. At this time, he also changed his management from TMG to Edward White and Co., LLP in Woodland Hills, California.

From this moment on, he started to realize that he was indeed paying exorbitant fees, and most of his monies had not been well-accounted for. He opted to file a lawsuit against TMG.

His financial woes started when he failed to sign a contract with TMG regarding their management fees, with nothing written about the percentage to be paid to them from his entertainment contracts.[45]

### *Investments*

Johnny Depp is a good example of a person whose laid-back personality extends to his financial life as well as his social one.

By now we should have acquired a clear picture of how Depp manages his money; it should be no surprise that he is not a particularly enlightened investor. His track record is poor, and on the occasions when investments did return a yield, the high fees his advisors took wiped out much of his profit.

If there were assets (non-current, to be specific), it would have been much easier for him to make additional income and even have more options to shelter those assets and income from excessive taxation. Besides, good investments would have appreciated substantially in market value over the past two decades. A careful investment program could have taken on headache out of his life.

He was a man with no clear financial roadmap of where he had initially come from and, where he was heading. He seemed not to recognize that what is spent cannot be recovered. Like many people, he seemed oblivious to the fact that he was not getting any younger, and most of the contracts on which he embarked were intended to guarantee him a better, if not the best, life when he finally retired.

He lost out because of the bad advice he received. The blame for this appears to lie, at least in part, with him. He left everything at his managers' disposal and shied away from tying up his contracts tightly. Lawyers may be expensive, but they are an investment well spent.

It seems as though bad advice might have accounted for half of the astonishing actor's accumulated wealth. Although he is hardly on the poverty line, with an estimated fortune of $165 million, he could be enjoying far more wealth. He may, of course, feel that his expenditure has been worthwhile, given his high earning potential, and the losses have been acceptable as a return on the life he has lived over the past three decades. We cannot know for sure, but certainly if we are taking his financial life story to illustrate the dos and don'ts of effective financial planning and investment, then we can learn from what we would, from our perspective, see as mistakes.

But we should never forget the astounding part of his story. Despite all his troubles, private dramas and financial disasters he is still a very wealthy man. With better advice in the future, and more controlled spending, he will remain as such. He can remain as the friendly pirate of society, the artistic rebel with a lavish lifestyle. He can enjoy his expenditure on everything from fine way to good causes spender for fine things and good causes.

Perhaps Johnny Depp adheres to the principle that we cannot take our money with us, so let us enjoy it while we can. This might not be a good model for financial planning…but it sounds a lot of fun.

## *Comparing Jennifer Lawrence with Johnny Depp*

Both Depp and Lawrence are unique entertainers. They have stamped their personalities on the movie world. Both live at the apex of modern-day acting careers. They have earned the best scripts, which they turn into amazing movies through their astonishing acting skills. Both Depp and Jennifer Lawrence are A-list performers. Both were born in Kentucky. (We are not suggesting a link between these points!) Both of them have played significant roles in the on-going development of the entertainment world and especially through their personal acting careers. They have won many accolades and much praise through the Academy Awards and Golden Globe Awards. Each has been defined as the best actor or actress in his or her specific categories.

Yet, in other ways, they couldn't be more different. Depp, the older, more established actor; Lawrence, the young, rebellious actress. It is their personalities, value systems and relationship towards money that takes them worlds apart.

### *Public Image*

Depp is widely known for his opulent lifestyle. He has always been open about his excesses. Some of the things in which he has engaged are simply mind-boggling and bizarre in the extreme.

For example, he blasted Thompson's ashes into space over Aspen, Colorado, at the cost of $3 million. With this and many more extravagancies (including spending $300,000 for exported wine for his personal consumption), the reason why he lost nearly half of his wealth is clear.

Jennifer Lawrence, on the other hand, early on reflected the image of a young girl from Louisville, Kentucky, who made it big in Hollywood—a typical rags-to-riches story. And her down-to earth style, with its typical Kentucky charm, allied to her conservative relationship towards money earned her another title: that of being the sensible starlet of Hollywood.

Even though Jennifer Lawrence has been the best-paid actress for several years in a row, she doesn't engage in the same "excesses" of flaunting her wealth and status as is often expected from a movie star of her rank. It's the smaller things and gestures that show Lawrence's down-to-earth character and her relation towards wealth and status. A good example is her not insisting on valet parking services or the obligatory "fruit basket." Even with her success, Jennifer Lawrence has remained humble.

## The Importance of Family Influences

It is believed that these seemingly old-fashioned values can be traced back to Lawrence's upbringing and the importance of her family. Jennifer Lawrence was brought up in a really loving and caring home. Her parents have been excellent mentors. They made sure that they inculcated sound financial practices in their children from a very young age.

Depp's family upbringing is much the opposite of Lawrence's. Being the youngest of the family siblings, he had to visit his father from time to time to collect the weekly child support money. His family never provided a check on their youngest's extravagances. The level of supervision that was given to the young Jennifer Lawrence was simply not there.

## Proper Advice

What could be interpreted by psychologists as a craving for attention manifested itself in Depp's relationship with money and his spending habits. Depp's opulent lifestyle includes a real reluctance to accept any value towards personal financial control. The kind of traditional family values that Lawrence so much enjoyed and that Depp lacked might have led Depp to trust people he shouldn't have.

While Depp might have been leading a lavish lifestyle, a big chunk of his earned fortune has been plundered through dubious management from his agency and advisors. Depp knowingly hired many assistants (management, personal lawyer/manager, agent). But whether they held their client's interests at heart is open to debate. In the end, Depp was misled by the very people with whom he had entrusted his fortune. Large salaries, unagreed loans—without doubt Depp's money was mismanaged, but a part of that blame must lie with his own lack of interest in putting proper processes in place.

Lawrence avoids using assistants and overly-eager advisors. Unusual for a woman in her position, she does not have a personal assistant to help in running her affairs. This omission reflects her own financial discipline, management and effectiveness.

Even though many people might consider her approach retrograde (why do something yourself if you can pay another to do it for you?), Jennifer Lawrence's attitude towards her financial management stands out among the pack of A-list Hollywood stars. She has maintained her sense of financial reality over time, something in which Depp appears to have failed miserably. While things can, of course, change, Jennifer Lawrence's firm and basic values are serving her well.

She has remained a person living within her means (as considerable as these are), who takes responsibility for her actions. This applies to both her career and private finances.

She wants to live a life that inspires others, and one which others can imitate.

Depp, as talented and adorable as he is in his movies, offers us a vastly different view of wealth and fame. Sometimes, he can appear as the archetypal movie star—the one who goes from rags to riches and back again (relatively speaking). The kind who allows it all to go to his head. Then again, he is a man who broke free from tough beginnings, who allowed his astonishing talents to break the chains of his early life. Perhaps he feels he deserves his lifestyle.

## Chapter 3
## SPORTING ICONS

Once upon a time, sport was the haunt of the amateur, something men (and sometimes women) played after work had finished for the week. It was popular—not just with the players but also with those who gained their entertainment from watching their heroes.

But heroes have a value, and over the last century, the growth of professionalism spurted up from the soil of amateurism. Joe DiMaggio, Billy Jean King, John McEnroe, O. J. Simpson, Michael Johnson, Tiger Woods, Michael Jordan. Mike Tyson to Cristiano Ronaldo.

They are the "Galácticos" in their respective sports, but too many times their private lives are peppered with failure, embarrassments and pure financial blunders—much to the amusement of the public. But there are astounding and inspirational exceptions—contrary to widely believed stereotypes within the sports industry, and that counts for both success and financial failure.

Sports players do not just make their income from their prowess on the field, around the track or in the ring. Obviously, those who have exceptional skills in their field hold a great advantage over we mere sporting mortals, but we can still take lessons from them.

Especially the way that the financially most successful athletes diversify as their careers develop.

David Beckham was a good soccer player. Talented, but certainly not a great. However, as well as a particularly fine right foot, he had two additional assets. These were astonishingly good looks and a superstar wife. Beckham was vilified as a young player. His naive over-reaction to a tackle saw him sent off in a World Cup match, effectively removing his country, England, from a tournament they may well have won.

Yet, through good advice, promoting his looks, and manipulating the extensive public interest in his marriage to a Spice Girl, he has made himself financially extremely rich for life. He now holds financial empires, along with his wife, in fashion, cosmetics and perfumery, modeling and property.

However, he is not the subject of our chapter, merely another example of what we will now consider.

## LeBron James—King James

*"I'm going to use all my tools, my God-given ability, and make the best life I can with it."—LeBron James*

Today, perhaps the biggest name in American sport is LeBron James, a man who has taken an astonishing natural talent, allied it to a physicality that is exceptional, and turned himself into not just a national, but a global superstar.

But LeBron James is more than just a sportsman. Like many high-earning players, he is also a shrewd and successful businessman and investor. As his sporting career comes towards a glorious end, his business and financial interests occupy an ever-greater percentage of his time. Certainly, his work has earned an accolade from one of the most successful entrepreneurs on the planet—Warren Buffet.

In an interview with NBA TV, Buffett described LeBron as "remarkably mature," being "plenty smart about financial matters," and saying, "I was impressed with him right from the moment I met him."

James himself recalls the conversation between the two. "Warren Buffet told me once and he said, 'always follow your gut.' When you have that gut feeling, you have to go with, don't go back on it," he said.

### Upbringing and Career

LeBron James, King James, the pre-eminent name in the world

of basketball, the player many believe is the greatest in the history of the sport. The King has amassed a fortune worth over $300 million. Not bad for a kid brought up by a single mom in the tough city of Akron, Ohio.[46]

Indeed, James's early life was tough. Initially, although his mother was just a young kid herself, but with the support of a caring grandmother and loving great-grandmother, plus a large, rambling house to run around in, life seemed good.

But before he started school, both of these influences on his life died. He and his mother were forced onto the streets, unable to heat or maintain their home. They spent years staying for a couple of weeks at a friend's home, before moving on to another short-term pad. This was a kid who moved around as much in his early life as he does now on the courts over which he reigns. This was a crucial point in LeBron's life. He was getting into trouble at school, failing in his studies, developing an attitude (not least as a reaction to his height, which marked him out as different—something a child never wants to be). It looked as though James would be lost to the good side of society and end up among the gangs that patrolled Akron.

However, stability entered his life, moving him back onto the right side of the tracks, when a coach spotted his enormous sporting potential. From then on, like a playbook out of a Hollywood movie, everything changed and fell into the right places.

Firstly, this man, then another coach, took him into their family, providing the role models he needed. The money started to roll in as soon as he started playing professionally after finishing high school, leaving his education early so he could pursue his chosen career at a level consummate with his talent.

A pact entered with Nike when he was still in high school spanned seven years and earned him a staggering $90 million. His initial agreement with the Cleveland Cavaliers earned him $18.8 million for a period of four years when he was still an amateur. After 44 years of Nike's existence, it entered into its first "lifetime" deal. That too was with LeBron James.[47]

It was a contract that would see James earn over $1 billion. Based on the sales of James' trademark shoes, the deal began in December 2015.

In August 2016, he entered into another pact with the Cleveland Cavaliers; this would see him rake in earnings of $100 million over the next three years. Another record. James has a range of endorsement deals off the court. A nice supplement to his already enormous salary, by just promoting various companies' products including his own line of fashion items. Companies that have entered into promotion agreements with James include Kia Motors, Upper Deck, Coca Cola and Beats.[48]

From a business perspective, LeBron James is different from many other sporting icons in that he has diversified into fields that are not directly related to his sporting successes. While his salary, and the endorsements that come from his fame on the court, still account for a significant part of his earnings, when he finally retires from the sport, he will not see wealth slowly slip away as has been the case with many other great sports players.

With the best will in the world, fame is transient, and after a generation or two, the appeal of LeBron as a sporting role model will begin to fade. He will not attract the same level of sponsorship as he does today. But because he has used his business sense, and his willingness to listen to the advice of experts, he has entered many other investment fields, including food, leisure and entertainment.

For example, thanks to Blaze Pizza (James is one of the founders), the franchise chains are in 25 states in the U.S., and they are notably big sellers in Miami and Chicago. The company has trebled its sales (to $101 million) over the last couple of years.[49]

His investment in the entertainment industry through SpringHill Entertainment and another company, Uninterrupted, earned him a $15.8 million investment from Time Warner. This has gone a long way in establishing him as a force to reckon with in the media and entertainment industry. His companies produce hit series and shows including Survivor's Remorse and Cleveland Hustles.

But LeBron James is far more than simply a super talented basketball player with an eye for a business opportunity. His financial success goes way beyond the large salaries he is able to generate. Because James has another outstanding talent—as an entrepreneur and investor.

### *Learning from Mistakes*

LeBron dealings with friend and associate Maverick Carter has another lesson we can take here. Maverick Carter has not always offered the best advice. A case in point was the way in which LeBron James announced his move from the Cleveland Cavaliers in the early 2010s. James was already a superstar, winner of numerous MVP awards, and the most coveted player in the league.

He was also a hometown boy. His decision to ply his trade elsewhere was something totally within his rights. He had become a free agent, so he was not breaking a contract; as an Olympic Gold-winning athlete, he wanted to continue his career with a team that could become play-off champions, something just outside the reach of Cleveland at that time. (Something, as fans know, LeBron remedied during his second spell with the team.) So, he chose to move to Miami Heat, a Galactica of a franchise, and one that could deliver the world with LeBron on board.

For James, it offered further chance to promote himself and increase his earning potential, but more importantly, it gave him a chance for success. Something that drives the greatest sportsmen more than just money. All but the most blinkered of Cleveland fans would have understood this.

But the guidance he was offered in announcing that move was ill-thought-out. Appearing on an ESPN special during which, with bling and glitz, he announced that he was leaving his hometown team to join the superstars of Miami, was ill-judged. LeBron James was one of us, and we do not announce that we are changing jobs to trumpets and lights on national television.

Maverick Carter realized that an error of judgement had been made, and so he did everything possible in order to redeem James' career and ensure he struck the best deals in history. Ever since this PR debacle, LeBron has been careful how to treat his fans and the public. He understood that advisors make mistakes, too, and that he needed to take personal responsibility off the field as he did on the field. This understanding served him well, as he has continued a successful career in basketball, business dealings and very soon a new field: investing.

### *Learning from the Best*

James has always been passionate about his businesses dealings. But he has kept his mind clear as well. This clarity of thinking, not getting carried away by events, has served him well. He does not forget that his art is borne through constant guidance and inspiration from personalities who are known and respected all over the world. He seeks guidance and he seeks it from the best.

When LeBron started out learning about entrepreneurship and investing, the name Warren Buffett naturally came up as America's most successful and most famous investor.

Through his own initiative, LeBron sought advice from the Oracle of Omaha, and when the chance came in 2007, he stayed with Buffett for a weekend in Omaha.

"I sent an e-mail about this to Warren Buffett. I'm a kid from Akron who lived in poverty for a long time."[50]

Since then their relationship grew, with LeBron seeking regular council, sending emails back and forth, even sending his personal financial statements to "Uncle Warren" (which is what he respectfully calls the billionaire investor, and in return for his advice, he invites Buffett to many of his NBA games).

The respect for each other is mutual and grew over the years: Warren Buffet is reported to have said this about him, "He's savvy. He's smart about financial matters. It's amazing to me the maturity he exhibits."[51]

For LeBron, it goes beyond just mundane business or investment advice: "I had an opportunity to go and spend some time with him a few years ago and our relationship just continues to grow and grow and grow. On business and then personal stuff, as well. So, it's cool." James added.

It seems that even King James is not beneath good council nor learning from the leading experts in fields he is not King in. That truly makes a great king!

### *The Investor—Learning from the Best*

One of his first forays into this field involved his association with Beats. The reported sale of Beats Electronics to Apple is rumored to have earned him $30 million. Every businessman needs a big break; this can come when they get a profit from their array of assets, for example. LeBron James made a $4 million profit from the sale of his house in Coconut Grove. He had initially bought it for $9 million when he joined Miami Heat, selling it for $13 million when he decided (to huge public celebration in the north) to resume his career at Cleveland.[52] No doubt some of that additional value came from the reflected glory cast on the rich bidding for a house in which LeBron James had lived. In addition to these, James is a minority shareholder of Liverpool Football

Club, a deal he entered into with the help of Fenway Sports Group. Another wise move, it seems. Under the management of German coach Jurgen Klopp, the once mighty team has regained its status as one of Europe's leading clubs in this cash-rich industry.

Last season, Liverpool reached the Champions League Final, Europe's premier competition. This season, many are tipping them to regain the title for the first time since 1990, which marked the end of the dominance of domestic English and European football they had enjoyed for almost two decades.

As we can see, one of LeBron James' greatest assets is his superb timing. The value of Liverpool Football Club is about to go through the roof (just as what happened with his Miami home), and he is there to reap the rewards. Such timing, though, is not down to chance, but to shrewd observation of all the markets that hold interest to him, the development of strong connections in these markets, and the willingness to listen to and consider advice.

LeBron James has been categorical about how he invests his money. Close to his heart are family, personality, devotion, originality, and his hometown of Akron. These considerations inform the investment decision he makes.

His personal wealth is managed through his own marketing bureau, LRMR Management Company. This has made him stand out from the rest of his peers in the sports and entertainment industry, many of whom outsource this very critical function to other entities. This can mean that very intimate financial information and secrets lay in the hands of a multitude of different people. The potential for leaks, or risk to the money, is increased when it is controlled through third parties. In very bad situations, it might lead to manipulation and coercion from other competitors due to financial espionage.

In addition to this, LeBron James' former partner at LRMR was the turbo engine that propelled him to be big in his professional and business fields. He was the man behind every business deal and he negotiated all of these in a manner that was the envy of many.

James, therefore, associated himself with a key ally who has been pivotal in the creation of his enviable business status. He picked his most trusted friend from high school, who has guided him in securing some of the best investment moves of any sports player in history.[53]

### *Overcoming Adversity—The Social Pioneer*

As we alluded to earlier in the chapter, a facet that defines LeBron James' character is his tough upbringing. Born between Christmas and New Year in 1984, the first few years of his life were comfortable, if not salubrious. His single mom, Gloria, was just sixteen when he was born, and he was brought up in an extended family within a large, rambling house in Akron. But when first his great-grandmother, then shortly afterwards his grandmother, died, the toddler saw his world begin to crumble.

Gloria and her brothers could not meet the financial demands of the house, and soon she and her son were homeless, forced to spend time moving around between friends and family. LeBron was a demanding child; big for his age—too big to be comfortable in his body—and one to whom school meant little. It was only after he was spotted as a potential junior running back for a local youth football team that he began to develop a purpose.

When the coach, Bruce Kelker, offered the opportunity for Gloria and LeBron to move into the home he shared with his young wife, she jumped at the chance. That worked out well until Kelker and his wife were ready to move on, and then another coach, Frank Walker, offered nine-year-old LeBron a share of his son's room. Although there was no room for Gloria in the house, the arrangement worked out well. With strong role models, LeBron got back on track. Within a year, the ten-year-old had turned from miscreant to, if not exactly model pupil, one with a direction, at least.

The rest, as they say, is history. But history is only useful if we take note of it. And LeBron certainly has. As a globally renowned sportsman and a very rich man, he has two ways of spreading good. He takes advantage of both, mostly to give the best chance possible to kids in his home city of Akron.

LeBron uses his wealth and fame to promote many charities, and he has founded others. He holds regular counseling sessions where he talks with boys at risk of going off the rails. What could have more influence on a damaged fourteen-year-old than being addressed by a hero? Not only is the boy facing a physical specimen of great proportions, not only a leading sportsman but a man who knows exactly what it is like to grow up in a rundown city like Akron.

But perhaps most pertinent of all is the school LeBron finances through his charitable foundation. Fees, uniforms, tuition—all is paid for to give the needy the best chance in life they could have under the circumstances in which they live. Of course, it is a drain on his finances but, although this is not the reason for his charitable work, it does win him brownie points in other aspects of his financial life. It helps to promote him as a good man, one who cares and can be trusted. It provides goodwill, on which business plans often depend. Those are side benefits; LeBron undertakes his charitable work for the good of others.

While his sporting career is coming to an end, and whether he moves into media, coaching, full-time business, community work or a combination of them all, we can be pretty sure he will make a success of whatever he decides to do.

It is hard to think of many better examples of a person taking his greatest attribute, honing it to as close to perfection as can be imagined, and then using it as a stepping board to even greater glory—this time in his business enterprises. He personifies the importance of listening to others, taking advice, learning from mistakes and believing in himself. LeBron James, from poor boy to one of the richest men in the United States. While most of us cannot dream of possessing the physical skills of a man such as he, we can take the lesson of how he used one facet of his life—his basketball—to lead to success in another—his financial prowess.

## Dr. Hans-Wilhelm Müller-Wohlfahrt – Healing Hans

*"My problem is I work really hard and all day long, from early morning to night."*— Dr. Hans-Wilhelm Müller-Wohlfahrt

Dr. Hans-Wilhelm Müller Wohlfahrt (known as MW) is the most famous medical doctor in Germany. He is the doctor for sports superstars, and not only does he include numerous celebrities among his clients, but he has become one himself—a star of sports medicine.

For almost 40 years, he has been responsible for the leading German soccer team—and one of the best clubs in Europe: Bayern Munich. The accolades he gained at this club, his main employer, brought him the job of staff doctor of the German National team for over 20 years. Many consider this side to have been the strongest National soccer team of the era, one that won the World Cup twice in the period.

His client list reads like a "Who's Who" of sports stars and includes those from beyond this world. He has treated the elite of global pro soccer players. He has treated other celebrities from various sports, among them such superstars as Usain Bolt, Boris Becker and Katarina Witt. Even musical celebrities such as Bono of U2, Eric Clapton and Luciano Pavarotti have been his patients.[54]

Yet, there is a lesser-known side of MW. A character trait that brought him not only trouble with his closest friends, but also saw his personal financial situation crash.

While he might find glory, fame and recognition from his peers worldwide, he experienced personal failure and something close to financial ruin caused by an area over which he had neither interest nor control. Money.

## *Upbringing and Career*

The doctor was born as Hans-Wilhelm Müller on August 12th, 1942, in Leerhafe, today part of Wittmund, East Frisia. He is the son of a pastor and a housewife. During his high school days, he showed an interest in sports. He trained as an athlete and developed his personal sports and diet regime that he would refine and retain into his later years. Many who have seen him throughout his life believe he looks much younger than his age. Even today, at 76, he looks 20 years younger than a typical 76-year-old.

In 1963, he studied medicine in Kiel, Germany, a small city in the north of the country. Being interested in sports and general fitness, he specialized in orthopedic and sports medicine. With stints in Innsbruck, Austria, he completed his doctorate in Berlin, Germany, in 1971.

In 1975, after some low-level jobs, MW kick-started his career at Hertha Berlin, a moderately successful soccer team in Germany. He remained there until 1977, when he got a call from the best soccer club in the country: FC Bayern Munich, which is based in the nation's second city, further to the south. The best-known and most successful club in German soccer history needed a young staff doctor with energy and talent, and MW fit the bill.

Bayern Munich is a giant in soccer not only in Germany, but the whole of Europe. It was a glorious time for the club; they were the continent's pre-eminent team at the time, having won the European Cup for three consecutive seasons between 1974 and 1976, a feat accomplished only by one other club—Spain's Real Madrid.

No question, for MW it was his great chance, his big break. At that time, although he was still relatively inexperienced, MW excelled under the pressure that came from being at the top. He quickly made a name for himself among his patients, who recovered more quickly than expected when under his care, and top management, who saw their assets back on the field, performing as soon as possible after injury (and often, it seemed, sooner than that).

Then, in 1990, he received the ultimate accolade. The soon-to-be World Champions, Germany, needed a team doctor, and MW earned the position. Despite his sometimes controversial treatment methods, what he offered worked, and the world's strongest soccer team wanted those skills to keep their players fit and ready to play.

## *The Special Doctor*

Today, he is a world-renowned expert for sports injuries, especially in knee problems and tendon damage. His treatment methods have always been based on the simple and the natural. As he himself noted several times in interviews, "God has given me a gift," he sees and heals with his hands. No high-powered machine can diagnose a sports injury more precisely than the touch of MW. Though conventionally trained in medicine and orthopedics, his practice employs a unique mixture of homeopathic medicine (treatment with natural substances) and acupuncture.

The lifeblood of his treatments is what Müller-Wohlfahrt calls "infiltrations." These are homeopathic preparations and other substances that are injected into the injury site: exotic stuff like Actovegin, an amino acid preparation derived from calves' blood, and lubricating substances containing purified hyaluronic acid and antioxidants.

MW isn't an ordinary doctor. For many in the industry, he ranks as the greatest healer since Hippocrates. He gained the nickname "Healing Hans," a pun affectionately used by his patients when referring to him.

Over the years, he has gained an A-list of believers who have included Boris Becker, the German tennis ace, the soccer player Ronaldo, the late Italian opera singer and tenor, Luciano Pavarotti, the great German defender Franz Beckenbauer and, it seems, just about every major German soccer player since.

His early success brought him in touch with Dr. Richard Steadman, founder of the Steadman Clinic in Vail, Colorado, a leading sports orthopedic group. Their mutual respect for each other's work developed into a very successful partnership and personal friendship that has lasted for three decades. Dr. Steadman and MW share and refer high-profile patients back and forth across the Atlantic. They work together to provide both surgical and non-surgical treatment.

Through this connection, MW's reputation spread beyond Europe to the U.S. and the rest of the world. Sprinters Tyson Gay and Maurice Greene, as well as bad-boy skier Bode Miller, soon numbered among his clients.

For example, on one recent spring day, the patients MW treated included as diverse a mix as:
A world-famous lion tamer;
The editor of Cosmopolitan Magazine in Germany;
The CEO of Bayern Munich;
A couple of World famous Olympic athletes;
Oh, and a feisty 92-year-old woman!

And a combination of his training, experience, unique skills and bedside manner not only brought professional adulation, but financial benefits as well.[55]

## *Earnings, Income and Private Spending*

In Munich, MW led a happy life that he shared with his wife, Karin. They resided in a prominent area in the center of the beautiful city. They have two children: a daughter, who is now married and lives in Sicily, and a son, a medical doctor himself, who works with MW in his medical practice in Munich.

In his private life, he enjoyed the fruits of the upper-middle class—the educated and learned who are most often associated with the arts and cultural traditions. MW has always been interested in art and architecture. His wife Karin is a self-proclaimed artist mingling with the leading artists of the Munich scene. MW is also passionate about classical music, still playing the trombone and organ occasionally. He cycled and continues to do so, every day in the morning from his apartment to his clinic.

MW had found the perfect balance of family, fulfilling work and professional recognition. But, with the commercialization of European Football starting with David Beckham in the late 1990s and the fame that went along with this, things started to change.

MW is not a showman; he is not a darling of the media, nor a member of the sound-bite generation. Despite his dramatic, flowing locks, he is not a person who courts celebrity; rather, it is something that his talent saw thrust upon him. In fact, MW is quite a shy man, comfortable with his patients and his family, but not so under the glare of media attention. But the era brought a new reality with which, at times, MW found it difficult to cope.

Initially, he maintained a small, inconspicuous office in Fürstenfelder Strasse in Munich. But his rising fame and success meant that it was time to upgrade. In May 2008, he moved his office to one of the most prominent addresses in Munich—Alten

Hof—an idyllic place in a 12th century Gothic structure that served as the first imperial residence of Ludwig the Bavarian. It lies between Marienplatz and Maximilianstraße in the heart of the city.

Rents in this location can often fetch over 10,000 euros per square meter, and taking on that space would cost MW about €40,000 ($47,000) per month. Naturally, the space needed an upgrade to be worthy of a leading sports physician. With an area of over 1,650 square meters, the star architect David Chipperfield was given the freedom to unfold his genius. The resulting upgrade cost € 700,000 ($820,000).[56]

Key players from a more modern Bayern Munich era, like Franck Ribery, Arjen Robben and Philipp Lahm, arrived. This meant four- or five-digit sums for each treatment. Invoices for several million euros were written for all the sports and boulevard celebrities who frequented his clinic.

His fees charged to Bayern Munich alone generated up to half a million euros annually, and he received undisclosed compensation from the DFB, the ruling body which oversees the German National Team. The income stream MW enjoyed was growing all the time.

With an ultra-modern and high-tech clinic located on the best address in Munich, the most impressive sports clientele for whom a doctor could wish and two employers who were giants in their respective field, the potential was there to give the good doctor all the honors and wealth he could wish for.

But the money began flowing out as quickly as it came in. His clinic employs two doctors (including his son) who, in line with their talents, both receive competitive salaries. Although MW prefers a quiet existence, his wife Karin, the artist, does enjoy a celebrity lifestyle that is largely funded from her husband's work. His married daughter, Maren (now living in Sicily), received regular financial support. He also maintained a house in the south of France.

Surely, he and his wife had good taste. They deserved and enjoyed a lifestyle becoming of a doctor of such status attending such a high-level clientele. And the large income MW made justified the couple's spending. Plus, a lot of that expenditure was geared towards upholding the sort of image that celebrities and wealthy clients would expect from their elite doctor.

But occasionally, spouts of doubt and fear over retirement flooded into MW, a trait not unknown in the rich and successful

German society. In Germany, it's called "Ur-Angst," an angst particularly related to an elementary fear of not having enough money. And worse, an irrational fear of how a person without the ability to sustain their lifestyle might be perceived by their neighbors.

MW realized he needed to do something beyond his career—something that would secure his status—an iron-clad retirement plan that went beyond the ordinary pension, a source of money he could employ to keep himself and his family happy. So, MW became open to the birds singing into his ears for easy money... and whole flocks of birds sang a new song—the song of MW becoming an entrepreneur and businessman.

### *Great Doctor—Failed Businessman*

Already in 1998, MW founded the Formula Müller Wohlfahrt Health and Fitness AG. The aim of the joint stock company was the development, the production and the sale of pharmaceuticals, dietary supplements and personal care products. It was supposed to be the original retirement plan MW had been dreaming of.[57]

MW controlled 50% of that company together with his son, Kilian. The remaining 50% was spread among his friends and famous people. Franz Beckenbauer, the German football legend, held shares and Franz Prinz von Auerberg did as well. Also, the monied Munich nobility was represented: the former media entrepreneur Thomas Haffa, the Bavarian bathing king Johannes Zwick, plus a rich sheik from the Middle East, Omar Qandeel. They all saw the opportunity for investment.

MW came up with many types of ideas: a cooling spray, taping products, and so forth. A blockbuster of a commercial winner should have been Profelan, a pain cream made with arnica flowers, the herbal remedy. Early investors, who strongly encouraged him to venture out beyond his day job as a doctor, were thrilled. You could see the dollar signs in their eyes and they already heard the cash registers ring.

But after that initial euphoria, earnings were more than disappointing. Sales became lackluster and the years of small profits were followed by as many that saw a loss. What was needed, everyone believed, was a big investor with big money. One that would push this business to a higher level. Somebody who could make the investment that would bring international recognition and growth this business deserved.

The person who could make that vision reality was Dietmar Hopp, the retired billionaire founder of SAP SE and now a philanthropist. The many causes he supports include sports development, medicine and education. The match between Hopp and MW seemed perfect.

Together the billionaire and the celebrity doctor registered a separate company called MW Group, with an office in Heidelberg, and the MW Center for Orthopedics and Sports Medicine in Munich. Hopp was supposed to be the anchor investor—the key man who would act as a magnet to attract more investors to the business.[58]

In glossy brochures, the MW Group was promoted as the world's leading sports clinic. Advertising jargon such as "Know-how MW" with "MW preparations" were employed. The business' range of supplements and lotions were directly developed and provided by the celebrity doctor himself, said the marketing material.

By employing this strategy, sales should gush in. Growth rates and profits margins would water every investor's mouth. MW and MW Group would become a global brand, used by elite sports stars and the many followers who strived to be like their sporting heroes.

Convinced of the potential, Dietmar Hopp made a large investment of € 7 million ($8.2 million) for the first clinic—Alter Hof. It would be the starting point for something much bigger. Like the "patient zero" in medicine, the first clinic in Munich would be the core in a network of clinics around the globe, replicated from the early successes of the first. The opening of the clinic in 2008 was the business milestone for which every investor and shareholder of MW's company had wished.

But Hopp and other investors noticed that Müller-Wohlfahrt was less than a cooperative business partner. From the start, MW showed very little interest in business affairs, such as lengthy business meetings, strategy planning sessions or simple administrative work. He was a doctor, not a businessman.

But at the same time, conversely, he wished to be involved in all strategic developments. No decision could be made without his direct consent. The result was constant delays, expensive mistakes and frustrated business partners and investors. According to one investor, "Every strain on an athlete is 100% more important." This almost fanatic conviction of "patient first" was good for his patients but bad for his investors. The high expectations investors had held were not achieved, and global expansion plans were canned very quickly. In 2013, both entities were bankrupt on paper and MW's personal relationship with Dietmar Hopp became severely strained.

According to official filings, the balance sheet for 2013 had a deficit in millions, without any equity remaining. Losses had already been incurred a year earlier. There were also demands made on the company from the Social Security Fund and legal teams.

Nevertheless, the business kept on going, because investors were concerned about their reputation and MW's (nobody likes to see their hero fall), so they kept the company alive quarter after quarter—but barely so, as though it was a patient on life support.

Perhaps MW should not have been surprised that he struggled to manage the multiple millions of euros in his company, because he had similar problems with his personal finances.[59]

### *Investment Errors and a Victim of Fraud*

In the aftermath of the subprime crisis, MW's wife Karin took the initiative to protect the wealth that still remained in the family, and so she sought out new investments. Something to allow them to diversify in risk-free opportunities but would yield comfortable returns. By sheer coincidence, a friend in Munich recommended a prominent investment advisor, who promised 30% returns without any risks. Her friend already had great success with this advisor and without any further due diligence, she invested half a million euros. Her first two dividends were paid promptly, and everything seemed to be fine, just like the investment advisor promised. Unfortunately, nothing more followed. Within a few months, the money was lost in a commodity-type investment scam.

Apparently, she and her friends became victims of a very basic form of a Ponzi scheme that went around among the rich and famous in Munich. As with any Ponzi scheme, it imploded as soon as new investors wouldn't sign up and the first signs of doubts about its propriety arose. The investment advisor concerned was sentenced to a prison term, but to MW's dismay, their money was gone.[60]

Besides blaming the fraudsters, Karin Müller had an easy explanation for her financial disaster. In a widely-watched German talk show, she admitted: "The money transactions are overseen by a tax accountant. Neither my husband nor I care—that's why." To give it a bit more gravitas, she followed up with a widely-believed German stereotype, "Artists and doctors are just those people who do not care about money."

But this indifference and blind trust in friends' recommendations and advisors would soon lead to even greater embarrassment for the couple than the Munich Ponzi scheme. Widely published and discussed in the German boulevard press, Karin provided a detailed account of their financial Waterloo.

Shortly after the Ponzi scandal, it was time to check the family's finances in more detail. Their initial retirement planning, based on MW becoming a successful entrepreneur, was already laid to rest by early 2014. And a half-million euro loss wasn't peanuts—not for the MWs.

What they would find out would bring pale faces, fury and wrath to the MW family, as they were informed that their long-term tax and legal counsel, somebody they saw as a friend, had cheated them for years. Hiring an outside forensic accountant, it was quickly deduced that about € 7 million ($8.2 million) were missing.

The final report was even more devastating. Apparently, MW had given his tax and legal counsel complete power of attorney, with access to bank accounts.

After further investigation, the new accountant realized that 11 legal entities were registered domestically and abroad to "optimize" tax payments and to manage MW's investments. What really happened at these legal entities no one knows, but profits and assets were nowhere to be found. One piece of advice that seemed to have some value was a warning to MW that his spending was excessive and needed to be cut. It might have been good advice, but it was expensive; the so-called friend had been charging the MWs a monthly flat-rate commission of € 11,900 per month ($14,000) for years.[61]

By the end of 2014, it was time to face up to the financial problems they had endured and to dare to make a restart. They hired a new legal counsel from one of the most prominent law firms in Munich, who referred MW to reputable tax and investment advisors. It would be the beginning of a lengthy recovery process—mentally as well as financially.

That year, MW celebrated his 72nd birthday, an age where most Germans enjoy the fruits of years of hard labor, playing golf and watching soccer. Not MW. In 2018, at the age of 76, he still works, and some say harder than ever. In his particular field, no one comes close to his experience, or his skill. He still loves his work. He knows no one can ever take that away from him.

## Comparing LeBron James with Hans Müller-Wohlfahrt

Both LeBron James and MW perform their professional duties at the highest level in their respective fields. Professional sport is about supreme performance, and in their own ways, each is at the top of their game. This is true whether we are speaking of LeBron, the basketball superstar, or MW, the superstar among sports physicians.

Their individual talents, but also dedication, drive and passion for their profession, allowed them to achieve the fame and recognition they deserve. In turn, fame translated into high income—or maybe it was their huge incomes that contributed to their fame. Through a detailed study of their lives, we can see how success really appears to those who have it in abundance.

Yet, each couldn't be more different when it comes to the life beyond their profession. LeBron from Akron, a black man from a poor neighborhood fighting for his early financial survival. MW, a white male and a superbly educated medical doctor, from a middle-class upbringing. One thing is clear: MW never experienced the social discrimination or even financial distress that LeBron must have experienced in his youth.

But when it comes to managing money, it seems that their lives are in reverse. The highly-educated, well-mannered and talented doctor has, at times, endured serious financial problems. In contrast, the kid from the rough neighborhood, known as a bad boy on the field, succeeded not only in his profession but also as an entrepreneur and money manager.

We all know the horrific examples of famous sports superstars of their personal failures and financial blunders. Examples range from Mike Tyson in boxing to Boris Becker in tennis. A recent case in England illustrated this perfectly. Alan Hudson was the soccer-playing equivalent of these two in his day, a super-talented player performing at the highest level. Now in his sixties, he is homeless and destitute. Paul Gascoigne was the star of the 1990 World Cup; now he is constantly in and out of treatment centers, living on the edge and the kindness of many friends who have made a life after sport. If any sporting star seemed likely to fall, it would be LeBron James.

Yes, LeBron leads an extravagant lifestyle with spending habits that seem excessive to us pure mortals. He regularly shows off his wealth on his Instagram feed—a collection of toys, expensive designer goods and the exotic places to which he travels. And nothing is wrong with that. He can afford it, as his income justifies his spending. Besides, these days, clever marketing strategies monetize an extravagant lifestyle—just ask the Kardashian/Jenner sisters. It's all about staying relevant to marketers and fans alike. And, in LeBron's case at least, paying back some of his own fortune through the charitable institutions he founded and supports.

The same applies to MW. Though leading a life not as flashy as LeBron, MW and his wife have been leading the good life among sports stars and celebrities. Now, as members of an educated and cultured upper-middle class society, comes a status that needs to be financed. Yet, this wasn't their financial ruin.

It is something much more potent about his personality that caused those financial concerns for MW. He simply holds no interest in money; he makes vast sums but has neither the skills nor the will to turn this into even greater income. He tried, but failed.

MW might be a miracle doctor in his profession, achieving great success, acclaim and fame, but when it comes to managing his private wealth or being the entrepreneurial type, he has failed. That is fine; not everybody wants to become a financial whizz-kid. Perhaps the lesson is that, not having the desire nor the interest to move into this field, he may have been unwise to have tried it. Or perhaps not. If money is something that doesn't especially matter to a person, then sometimes the experiences gained in life—even the bad ones—are worth the cost.

The reason for each of their financial outcomes is rather simple, although biographers might tell us otherwise. LeBron James was dedicated, curious and interested in managing money. He studied it, spent time and effort on it. From his success in basketball, he transferred his winning formula to business and money management. The most illustrative example is LeBron James' own initiative to consult with the best. He called out to Warren Buffett, and rather publicly celebrated the relationship of which both are proud.

On the other hand, MW would hide behind a façade of old social beliefs. As in many closed and conservative cultures, one does not talk about money in Germany. In that culture, among a certain generation of people, having a profession is not necessarily conducive to being a good manager of money.

What worsened the whole situation for him and his wife was their poor judge of character. They trusted friends and referrals blindly, without checks and balances. But then, MW and his wife seemingly had, and still have, little or no interest in managing their money. Perhaps they learned their lesson of not trusting advice—even from friends—without carrying out due diligence. One suspects that theirs was a mistake that LeBron James would not make.

LeBron James, from poor boy to one of the richest men in the United States. While most of us cannot dream of possessing the physical skills of a man such as he, we can take the lesson of how he used one facet of his life, his basketball, to lead to success in another—his financial prowess.

# Chapter 4
# LATIN AMERICAN TYCOONS

South of the US-Mexican border exists a parallel universe. Countries with enormous natural resources and fascinating cultural histories, but also with a bloody past, political coup d'états and ongoing and economic unrest. Central America and South America are seen as a hinterland in the West. Regions devoid of progress, cultural and political sophistication. Yet these are values from a Western perspective, and by opening our eyes we can all learn a great deal.

As we look at two more contrasting figures from the business world, Carlos Slim and Eike Batista, it is to this region that we turn. Each of these men was once among the top ten wealthiest people in the world and were famed in their own country and beyond. One remains a figure of admiration; the other lounges in relative poverty, a prison sentence served, his world collapsed; his empire gone. A modern Ozymandias:

> *"Look on my Works, ye Mighty, and despair!*
> *Nothing beside remains ..."*

## Carlos Slim—The Cash Machine

*"With three work days a week, we would have more time to relax; for quality of life."* —Carlos Slim

As The Telegraph once noted, Carlos Slim is "Possibly the richest man you've never heard of." A native of Mexico with a family empire controlling more than 200 companies spanning everything from banking to retail to telecoms to road building to restaurants. For most of his career, he remained unknown to much of the world. His fame was restricted to an elite circle of deal makers, politicians and businessmen.[62]

Carlos Slim was once the world's richest man, leaving even the likes of Bill Gates and Warren Buffett in his wake, but due to a declining value of the peso and losses at some of his key holdings, he has slipped in the global rankings. As of 2018, his wealth had shrunk to a mere $61.7 billion, making him #7 on the list of the super wealthy. That is a figure that nevertheless represents approximately 7.5% of his home nation's gross domestic product.

But given the size of his fortune, he has remained conspicuously frugal. Do not expect to see him in the bays of the Mediterranean, or on the shores of the Caribbean at home in a conspicuously ostentatious yacht. No GPS device is needed to navigate the corridors of his home. He won't appear on the grid at a Monte Carlo Race with supermodels on each arm.

In fact, he resembles more a person from a higher-middle income background with traditional family values. He appreciates the old bourgeois importance of education, hard work and frugality. His interests are those of the normal citizen, rather than a member of the elite. Most likely, in his leisure time, he will be exploiting his love of baseball rather than indulging in the pastimes of the rich.

But he does enjoy some of the trappings of wealth. Over time, he has developed a pristine interest in fine art. He is considered the world's foremost collector of Rodin sculptures. Carlos Slim is also one of the great philanthropists of the world, and he is an open critic on how Gates and Buffett handle their philanthropic affairs, saying, for example: "(Bill) Gates has to study how he can (fight poverty) in the same way that Microsoft...succeeded in business, because charity has not solved the problem."

Fame and recognition, probably unwanted, only came to him following a small investment in that "bastion of liberal America,"— small by his own standards; $250 million might make more of a dent in the pockets of most people.

### *Upbringing and Career*

Carlos Slim was born on January 28, 1940, in Mexico City to a family of five siblings. His parents were Linda Helu and Julian Slim Haddad, who were both of Lebanese descent. His father had already accumulated some wealth through opening dry goods stores in 1911 and 1921. Through his income, he invested in real estate in a commercial district of Mexico City, providing a comfortable upbringing for his family. Also at that time, he was an influential member of the Lebanese-Mexican business community, in which he remained an active and influential force until his death in 1953.

Carlos Slim had a largely comfortable upbringing. Although he was sometimes bullied for his Lebanese roots, within his family he grew up well-protected, something that taught him not only the values of family (something so important in Mexico), but old-fashioned tenets regarding education, hard work and frugality.

His father introduced him to business management at an early age. He learned the principles of good business practices, such as bookkeeping and investing. Early on in his life, he would be putting those lessons to the test. At the age of just 11, he invested in government saving bonds, keeping a detailed ledger to track all his purchases. By 15, he had bought a very small shareholding in Banco Nacional de Mexico—then the largest bank in Mexico.

At age 17, he worked for his father's company for 200 pesos per week, learning yet another lesson regarding the values of organization, teamwork and reliability.

When it came time to select an academic education, Carlos Slim chose to attend the National Autonomous University of Mexico, where he studied engineering. Even then, he was working hard and making some money on the side. He taught linear programming and algebra to younger students, earning a little pocket money for himself.

But it would be his private investments, which really inspired and drove him to excel, that would determine his future career. He understood early on that a traditional career in civil engineering was out of the question. He knew that his future lay in business ownership and shrewd investment. He finished his course, graduated, and followed his dream.

As soon as Slim finished his degree, he set up his own stock brokerage firm using a combination of the money he had saved and support from his family. There he worked 14-hour days in order to grow his business and his network. His eye was always looking out for the next deal.

It was almost as though he was following the script of Oliver Stone's iconic movie Wall Street. As a stockbroker, he had direct access to the rich and wealthy of Mexico and he was on the pulse of Mexican business trends. Such a position was a huge advantage in his search for investment opportunities. The young and ambitious businessman was finding the world to be good, and Slim thrived in it.

With the help of his client network, he invested in a number of business deals that included restaurants, retail, manufacturing and construction. He found he was mirroring the work of modern private equity funds more than that of a stockbroker. With each deal, he broadened his business network, his business acumen, and his skills as a deal maker. This would come in handy later in his career.

By 1966, at the age of just 26, he was already worth $40 million in today's terms. His next step was to expand into real estate by founding Immobiliaria Carso, following a path that his father took but on a much larger scale. The resulting growth spurt in his personal holdings stayed with him for many years, his developing business concerns matched by Mexico's growing population and economy. By 1972, he had already a diversified business empire that ranged from retail to real estate, to mining companies to printing businesses.[63]

In 1980, he consolidated and streamlined his existing business interests into a new company, called Grupo Galas (today as Grupo Carso). The move demonstrated his excellent intuition in recognizing changing trends and business timing—others would simply call it luck.

### *The Opportunity*

1982 was the year that gave Slim his big break—that once-in-a-lifetime chance he had been seeking for so many years. It was an eventful year for his country as well, although unfortunately for entirely less positive reasons. For Slim, 1982 was the year that saw him define his investment philosophy and set his company's DNA for decades to come.

Though already wealthy for his age, and despite his comfortable family background, that year Slim made real money by playing in the big league of Mexico's business elite. He took advantage of a nationwide "fire sale" of assets by local and foreign investors alike, looking to sell in the midst of one of the country's worst economic crises.

In August 1982, Mexico was the first of many Latin American countries to default on its sovereign debt. The Mexican economy contracted rapidly as many banks struggled and foreign investors left the country in droves. It was a real crisis of the peso, the local currency of Mexico. It lost value so rapidly that many businesses were unable to repay their US-denominated debt and were forced into bankruptcy. The subsequent years of recession were difficult for the country and its people.

During this time, Slim was in his element. With cash accumulated from his existing business interests, he started buying and investing heavily in Cigatam, a Mexican tobacco company, at what some experts called "fire sale" prices.

He ended up controlling the company, and he continued using its cash flows to buy more Mexican assets at low prices. The cigarette business proved to be a goldmine and cash cow; after all, who wants to give up smoking during a stressful recession?

With his combined cash flows, he acquired interests in chemicals, manufacturing, retail operations, food, and financial services. In effect, he bought a basket of the finest companies in all of Mexico—a premium version of the country's economy carefully chosen on the basis of quality and future potential. His boldness and eye for value laid the foundation for his future success as he catapulted himself on the landscape of Mexico's business elite. Only eight years later, he would demonstrate the same qualities once more, at a higher level and for higher stakes.

## *More Opportunities*

The second major turning point in Slim's career came in 1990. Mexico decided to privatize its national telecoms company.

Slim went head-to-head with America's Southwestern Bell, France Telecom, and as many as 35 other domestic investors. In the end, he won and seized control of Telmex, overcoming considerable competition and objections by opposing politicians.

Today, some 90% of the telephone lines in Mexico are operated by Telmex. But with his purchase of the company, he gained access to a far more important business interest—America Movil. With this, he gained access to one of the hottest and fastest growing business operations of the 21st century. He would soon expand operations into parts of Latin America's growing mobile phone market. Today, America Movil can be found operating in 11 countries, including Brazil, Ecuador and Guatemala, boasting in excess of 153 million customers.

Again, Slim demonstrated not only his financial genius, but also his boldness in undertaking substantial risk when the time was right. He saw through an aggressive deal-making plan, outwitting the likes of Bell and France Telecom. His boldness paid off, and it became his single most important investment—which to this day represents the core of his financial empire. Ultimately, it placed him on the global map that later allowed him to invest in the world most prestigious newspaper—The New York Times. It was a relatively small but highly symbolic move which came to represent a typical Slim investment.

## *A Chance in the United States*

Recent times have found Slim expanding into North America and even Europe. He has a tried and trusted method that works, and he always follows his own business handbook to the letter, operating on the basis of financial strength and grasping opportunities when they present themselves. Probably, the best example of this strategy remains his investment in The New York Times.

In late 2008, Slim took a 6.4% stake valued at $27 million in the then troubled New York Times Company, called by its fans and admirers "the Gray Lady," referring to the paper's circumspection as well as its conservative design and typography dating back to the 1950s. The news hit like a bombshell in the intellectual world of the old East Coast newspaper guild and caused anxiety among their liberal defenders.

How did circumstances arise to let Slim, virtually unknown at that time and from a country that is considered America's hinterland, in on the East Coast media action? Firstly, the global recession and declining advertising revenues took a particularly heavy toll on print-based "old media" companies across the United States. The New York Times was particularly vulnerable. It faced a liquidity crunch as a $400 million loan was about to mature in 2008, with global capital markets at a completely frozen state. The august old bird was struggling for funds. It had no choice but to accept the Mexican's money, and Slim had plenty of it!

Slim essentially bailed out the troubled company with a $250 million loan that came, as you might expect from him, at very good terms. According to The Financial Times, the bonds he received paid a 14% coupon that included warrants representing 16 million shares, with a strike price that was close to where New York Times shares traded in 2009.[64] By 2009, Slim had increased his stake to nearly 17%, becoming the single largest individual shareholder in The New York Times.[65]

Fast forward to December 2017. It was announced that Slim had sold half of his investment in The New York Times, marking the end of his foray into the Wall Street limelight. And even though he still owns half of his original investment, the initial investment itself was a stunning success.

Today, The New York Times is one of the few newspapers to have experienced a remarkable turnaround in business fortunes. The company restructured its balance sheet and sold off non-essential interests, such as The Boston Globe, while at the same time it invested aggressively in modern media, technology and marketing resources.

His initial investment plus the shares he received from exercising his warrants have almost quadrupled in value since January 2009. Slim cashed in on some hefty capital gains alongside the already mighty coupons he initially collected back in 2009.

His investment in The New York Times is a textbook case study on how Carlos Slim has been conducting his business and investment affairs and what he looked for in an investment opportunity. The broader news media might still be struggling financially in 2018, but according to The Financial Times, "the Gray Lady is thriving, critically and commercially."

## Decorum and the Elder Statesman

During one of his interviews with a British newspaper, he was asked for the secret to his success. He said that it stems from his admiration for his father Julian, who made his own fortune investing in property in the 1910-1917 Mexican revolution. It was his father who taught Slim the ins and outs of business management and proper work ethics.

It was not only the inspiration of his father that led him on this career path. He had also, since early childhood, found a role model in the brilliance of another business leader—J. Paul Getty, the American oil billionaire.

The first time Slim got to know Getty the oilman and international jetsetter was in 1965. This was no personal meeting, but insights from a column in Playboy magazine, where Getty wrote about the secrets of his success. Getty later published this collection of columns in his own book under the somewhat understated title, How to Be Rich. In the book, Getty urges his readers to cultivate a "millionaire mentality," which he describes as being "always and above all cost-conscious and profit-minded."

It made an impression on the then young Slim, and ever since he proceeded to mirror Getty's image. Slim learned of Getty's business acumen as a young boy and used it very successfully in his own wealth making. Slim noted, "I went from being an investor to being mainly an operator." A small but very subtle difference to many other operators who fail to distinguish between opportunity and outright gambling. This is a point worth keeping in mind when we discuss the second personality. It pays to have the right role models in life!

In a more recent interview with his biographer Diego Enrique Osorno, Slim revealed yet another surprising hero: the Mongol warlord Genghis Khan.

"Slim's fascination with the medieval emperor even reflects in his business strategies. Genghis Khan would make tactical retreats, lulling his enemies into a false sense of security, before striking hard," wrote the biographer.[66]

The tactics would come in handy, when over time his opponents grew with the size of his financial empire. But as tough as the Mexican is around the conference table, this hides a generous, loving and sensitive person, as we can see below.

### *Making Time for Family*

Just as his home is somewhat austere, Slim's downtown office in Mexico City's Lomas de Chapultepec neighborhood is similar, with tables full of papers and not a computer in sight.

On a corner pedestal sits "The Last Days of Napoleon," a sculpture by Vicenio Vela—a reminder that to keep your feet on the ground is a good piece of advice.

When not at work, he spends evenings with his family (his eldest son Carlos, a bachelor, still lives at home), enjoys lavishing time on his grandchildren, and uses any spare moments he has to write a book on his family. He likes to particularly focus on his father, of whom he is very proud.

But, in spite of his obvious wealth, he remains frugal in his tastes and is often seen wearing a plastic-effect wristwatch that doubles as a calculator, and his clothes tend to be bought from the many retailers his empire owns.

At weekends, rather than jetting around the world as he might, the widower told a recent interviewer that he likes to contemplate the dawn in Los Cabos, on the northwestern coast of Mexico, or wander around giant sequoia plantations.

With just six bedrooms and a small swimming pool, to an outsider's eye the dwelling looks somewhat simple, just like the furnishings that decorate the house's interior.

In fact, the only clue that this is no normal home is the considerable amount of fine art and sculpture that adorns it. Given its owner is the world's foremost collector of sculptures by Auguste Rodin and an avid collector of works by Renoir, Van Gogh, and Diego Rivera, from the inside, the house looks less like a residence and more like an art gallery.

Such frugality appears to be one of the reasons for his increased philanthropy. In spite of poking fun at fellow billionaires Bill Gates' and Warren Buffett's generous charitable giving—in March 2007 he said "our concept is more to accomplish and solve things, rather than giving; that is, not going around like Santa Claus"—he has committed to spending $10 billion through his charitable Carso Foundation over the next four years. Its main aim is to fight marginalization and poverty through investment in health, education and employment. "No one takes anything from this world when he dies," Slim said in 2007.

Slim is not without controversy and criticism, especially within his own country. There, according to a World Bank statistic, 50% of the population live below the poverty line. Such wealth as Slim possesses, even though it is never flaunted, is bound to raise jealousy in such circumstances. Although he has been accused of operating unfair business practices and at times of bribing officials, the main criticism is around not giving back enough of his personal fortune. This is not particularly fair, as he has dedicated himself (particularly later in his life) to charitable and philanthropic causes, but with less of the public fanfare than we are used to from the super-rich in the USA.

And even though his most recent biographer, Osorno, tries to put his enormous wealth into perspective by illustrating the darker side of Slim's business practices and growing empire, the most powerful picture a reader can take away from his biography is that of a "dignified and determined entrepreneur, a mathematical genius and dogged worker, who maintained a certain humility even as his wealth topped $77 billion."

As Osorno writes, the billionaire is now driven by the idea of victory more than actually making money. "He says he doesn't care about money," states the biographer, "He says 'This is my work, this is what makes my life make sense, what motivates me to get up. If they take this away from me, I would feel dead.'"[67]

At the age of 78, he has passed on most of the day-to-day operation of his business to his family, largely to his sons. They have shown great business acumen and talent themselves. But most importantly, his legacy is secure as his business values, and financial influences, live on through his family. His business achievements and personal wealth will continue to flourish long after he passes on.

Unfortunately, that cannot be said from the second person we will consider in this chapter, even though he, too, will have a place in the history books. Particularly those of his native country of Brazil—but, as we shall see in the following biography, his legacy will be of a very different kind.

# FORTUNES & BLUNDERS

## Eike Batista—The Brazilian Icarus

*"You cannot exist as a $20 billion company with speculation."*—Eike Batista

To many, he is the face of Brazilian capitalism, but for others, he is an eccentric, self-confessed megalomaniac. Controversy follows Eike Batista like a tail-wagging puppy.

He was once the richest man in Brazil—one of the most promising entrepreneurs of the world with a net worth of over $30 billion, ranking him at number 7 on the list of richest people in the world. He was included in the "50 Most Influential People in Global Finance" list in Bloomberg Markets. Batista once famously boasted that he would overtake Mexico's Carlos Slim to become the world's richest man by 2015.

He once had a fleet of luxury supercars, collecting them like children collect matchbox cars. He was married to a beautiful wife, but still enjoyed plenty of romantic entanglements with the sort of supermodels for which Brazil is famous. Even his prized possessions, his cars, shared his luxurious lifestyle, firstly his Mercedes and then his Lamborghini, parked not in the spacious garage, but in his living room. According to a tabloid magazine, he dined with the likes of Madonna and drank vintage champagne like water.

Batista had it all. He was on the top of the world, admired as one of the few persons "whose comments move markets; whose deals set the value of companies or securities; whose ideas and policies shape corporations, governments and economies."[68]

Yet today, he finds himself with a mountain of unpaid debt, possibly totaling more than $1 billion. He recently served a term in prison for bribery and perjury, seeing out his time in one of Brazil's most notorious prisons. He has been battling more lawsuits than a normal mortal could even imagine. Finally, he became entangled in corruption scandals, which formed a part of the much larger political troubles in Brazil. It's very unlikely that at age 63 he will ever return to his old glorious heights.

What had happened to a man who, like Carlos Slim, should have been destined as an elder statesman and representative of his country? A country that has been striving for more international respect and recognition, hosting the Olympic Games in 2012 and the World Cup in 2014. But, just like his native country in recent times, something seriously went wrong, and his life fell into a tailspin. In this biography, we will dive deeper into a life of risky deal making, fast cars, luxurious boats and, finally, total ruin.

### *Upbringing and Career*

B atista did not receive any inherited wealth. As he so many times emphasized, he was a "self-made" man. A man who built his wealth because of his own vision and boldness and his ability to develop and build important connections.

Eike Fuhrken Batista da Silva was born on November 3rd, 1956 in Minas Gerais, Brazil. Batista was the second of seven children. His parents were Eliezer Batista and Jutta Fuhrken, a native of Germany.

His father was an influential bureaucrat and important corporate director. As president of a state enterprise and former Minister of Mines and Energy in the João Goulart and Fernando Collor administrations, he provided a combination of political influence and upper-middle income for his family.

After spending his childhood in Brazil, Batista and his family moved to Europe, where his father's work took the whole family. As a teenager, he would spend his formative years together with his family in Geneva, Düsseldorf, and Brussels. When his father was called back to Brazil, Batista decided to stay behind and study at the prestigious engineering University of Aachen in Germany (RWTH Aachen), where he obtained a degree in metallurgical engineering. While he failed to complete his course, it still gave him the necessary training and theoretical knowledge that would underpin the start of his first business endeavor in Brazil.

When he returned to Brazil in 1979, he started out as a commodities trader, trying to export granite, marble and diamonds, and collecting commissions in the process. But in the early 1980s, another commodity caught his attention—gold. During this period, Brazil was under military rule and the Brazilin economy was both depressed and suffering from hyperinflation. In such circumstances, gold was in high demand. Seizing the opportunity, he turned into a dedicated gold trader. It was the right call and demonstrated the perfect timing of a master magician.[69]

That year, he convinced two gold traders in Rio de Janeiro to invest $500,000 in his new enterprise, one which saw him organize shovel miners in the Amazon to dig for gold. With the seed money, he started his own gold trading firm, "Autram Aurem," when he was just 23 years old—and this would become his first big break. At that age, he already had plenty of experience from trading other commodities, and he knew how to deal with and organize a rough group of garimpeiros (shovel miners).

He made a killing mining and selling gold, and he quickly raked up profits of about $60 million within less than two years. For his efforts, he took a 10 percent cut and thereby became instantly rich. It would be the beginning of a glorious growth story and a confirmation of Batista's conviction in the enormous wealth Brazilian natural resources had to offer to a man who held vision and ambition.

With the money he had made, he bought a mine and industrialized it. He gave it the name "TVX Gold." Supposedly, the X in the name stands for "multiplication," implying the multiplication of wealth. The mine he selected apparently turned out to be "idiot-proof" (as he later recalled). The phrase meant that it was enormously profitable no matter whatever the situation. It was a time of easy pickings for a man of his organization, skills and dash of daring.

TVX was just the beginning. In 1983, Batista founded the EBX Group, his future holding company and vehicle of choice under which he would organize all his future acquisitions and business dealings. But before the fantastic rise of the EBX Group, Batista got his first taste of adverse commodity price movement with TVX Gold itself.

Since acquiring the mine and renaming it to TVX Gold, Batista had created eight gold mines in Brazil and Canada, along with a silver mine in Chile. Six years on in his endeavors, he would be named CEO of the company he listed on the Canadian Stock

Exchange. His work with this provided a valuable experience he later replicated several times over. But not all went along as planned, and being a public company, he had to get used to more interference and scrutiny by investors as matters began to turn against him. It was not a situation he was used to.

In search of new mines to add to his growing conglomerate, Batista found an opportunity in Greece. But this time he over-dealt his hand; the mining business has never been for the faint-of-heart, even less so for the risk-averse investor. Batista was neither of these. Perhaps he soon wished he shared some of the traits of such people. His aggressive acquisition plans for a gold mine in Greece went awry amid political opposition and internal disagreements between his business associates from Greece and Russia and him. The Brazilian was outmaneuvered in a power struggle and was denied an environmental license from the Greek government for his mining project. He was left with a mountain of debt. He had invested heavily in preparation for taking on the mine and received the additional blow of gold prices falling to the historically low levels of below $300 per ounce.

His gold mining days were over! He had no choice but to resign as CEO and chairman of TVX Gold. He was no longer in charge of the company he founded—the company which marked the beginning of his success. Mr. Batista resigned in 2001, after his cash-strapped producer was forced to put itself up for sale. Soon after, TVX was bought out by Kinross Gold Corporation at fire sale prices. The value of gold then quickly recovered, once again reaching historic extremes—achieving a figure of nearly $2,000 per ounce in 2011.

After the debacle at TVX Gold, his attention returned to Brazil and to EBX. This was his early investment vehicle that he founded back in 1983. Between 2004 and 2012, he added six public companies under the EBX umbrella, including MPX (energy generation), MMX (mining), LLX (logistics), OSX (shipbuilding), and finally OGX (oil and gas), among many other acquisitions. Among these key procurements, OGX was by far the most important. It was soon to become his new cash engine—a jewel in the crown of his corporations that would catapult him into the company of the top 10 billionaires in the world.

How he financed such a spree of purchases after a major failure with TVX might be a mystery for the bystander, but the explanation for his continued success is quite simple. 2001 might have been the low point of gold prices and a year of temporary setback for Batista, but as the saying goes—double or nothing. This time, luck was on his side once more, and as the investment adventurist Jim Rogers observed, "It was the beginning of a major cycle in commodities."

What helped Batista to recover quickly was the performance of the assets he still owned and controlled—either himself or through his business network. Throughout his failure with TVX, he retained his charm and his salesmanship. He continued to gamble, albeit with other people's money. But they were quite happy to place their wealth in his hands—such was the confidence in his abilities.

With the change of the commodity megacycle, Batista floated shares from his conglomerate EBX through the BOVESPA stock exchange, the same schematics he learned and used with TVX Gold. With that, he had plenty of money with which to gamble... and gamble he did.

With the new commodities bull market raging, domestic and international investors caught the buying frenzy and bought everything from Batista they could lay their hands on. In this way, EBX was in a position to get capital, with debt holders and equity holders financing all its acquisitions from 2004 up until 2011.

In 2008, he was able to sell shares in MMX's three mines to Anglo American. He earned $5.5 billion in the process. A handy payout of pocket money! However, financial analysts speculate that this deal was more expensive than it might have been; indeed, it is reported to be one of his biggest deals. A sale of 22% of shares in MMX to China's Wuhan Iron and Steel for $400 million, and $700 million worth of MMX shares sold to South Korea's SK Networks together made him a fortune without having even extracted an ounce of iron ore.

He was earning substantial sums from mining, oil and gas production, ship building, logistics and energy. Then, in 2008, he put together another plan, correctly predicting the public disclosure of massive land deposits of oil reserves in his homeland.

His luck continued when these oil blocks were reserved for other investors. Batista made a fortune on the back of this investor frenzy between 2006 and 2010. Even following the Government directive regarding foreign investors, Batista continued to do well. He enlisted the help of OGX's former head of exploration, Paulo Mendonca, and made his own bid for oil blocks.

The bid was successful, with permission being granted to begin production in 21 flat deposits. This success turned OGX into the largest privately-owned oil entity in Brazil. Later that year, the company announced that it was aiming to produce more than one million barrels of oil a day by 2019. That figure would account for almost half of Brazil's total oil output.

The firm was indexed on the stock exchange in 2008, raising investment funds of $4.3 billion, a record for the time. Batista was raking it in.[70]

He had high dreams and grand visions for his growing empire. He was planning to build a "super port" in Rio de Janeiro, to be completed by 2013. It would be a hub—indeed, the hub—where the import and export of minerals and oil could take place. In many ways, his plans were to create a port similar to Houston's oil refinery sites. He was also quoted as "hoping to accumulate approximately $100 billion during the next decade."[71]

By 2011, EBX reached a market capitalization of over $40 billion. Eike Batista became the eighth richest man on the planet. It would mark the high point for Batista, as he wallowed in fame and glory. He was on his way to becoming a national hero and superstar in Brazil.

### *Spending: A Man Who Enjoys His Wealth*

With these lucrative deals under his belt, Batista proclaimed that he would be the richest man in the world in 2015 and be worth $100 billion by 2020; underpinning this would be his companies' $1.5 trillion of "underlying assets," which included the speculated amounts of mineral assets he owned in Mongolia.[72]

With his wealth regained, and entranced by his tendency towards publicity stunts, the media attention came, and that made him the iconic business guru he once was. But what really touched common Brazilians was his private life. He became what could be seen in today's terms as a kind of early internet viral success. In his way, he was as big a name as the soccer superstars that make Brazil the most exciting association soccer playing nation in the world.

When the news broke that he had become romantically entangled with supermodel, actress and carnival dancer Luma de Oliveira, the liaison became an instant sensation. According to the Brazilian version of People, the couple met in 1990 and were at the height of their romance. For Brazil, they were the Brazilian version of Brangelina, as they filled the gossip magazine's front pages issue after issue. Going forward, the media would have plenty to report about Batista's celebrated private life in coming years.

Being a media darling comes with certain obligations to justify such high standing. Batista, with his renewed wealth and fortune, once more began living the high life—he could afford it. He diversified into his love of power boating, winning several championship titles. Yachts, private jets and luxury mansions in Brazil's top spots (and the world over) also featured in his portfolio. One of his early prized possessions was a $1.2 million Mercedes-Benz SLR McLaren—the same one that he placed in his living room so that he could enjoy the beautiful lines of the car while watching soccer or the news. He added several more luxury cars in his growing fleet, including a white Lamborghini Aventador that would replace the Mercedes a few years later.

To make gossip columns even happier, Batista's marriage was followed by a messy divorce. During the divorce proceedings, it came out that he had affairs with a string of famous Brazilian socialites and supermodels. His marriage had lasted only 4 years. The couple had two children together, Thor and Olin.

Nevertheless, Batista was a man unaffected by his personal dramas. On the contrary, they increased his social following. Over the years, he proudly showed off his wealth. He traveled the world in his $61 million Gulfstream jet, gathering an eager entourage of loyal followers, each keen to hear his teachings. He was the J. Paul Getty of his day, the Donald Trump of his time, using whatever media was popular during those years to convey his story.

But there was a plan behind Batista's actions. They were not simply there to massage the ego of a super-rich man, or self-indulgence he was in a position to play out. With his frequent appearance in gossip columns and business interviews to proclaim his grand visions, he remained relevant to the public and business community. Banks loved him, many of them investing their own money in his projects. Stock dealers and other investors purchased and promoted everything that came out of Batista's financial behemoth.

The upshot of this media circus was that OGX had access to credit lines and cheap capital, helping it to expand aggressively. Interest came from both international and domestic banks, especially through BNDES, which lent OGX close to R$10.4 billion ($4.5 billion).[73]

Once again, his salesmanship and personal charisma proved to be decisive, but this particular approach to business was coming to the end of its useful life. This would prove to be the last time his charm offensive and celebrity lifestyle would work and convince creditors and investors alike that his business interests were worth their time and money. Batista was about to plunge downhill at speed Brazil's business elite had never seen before.

### *The Higher You Rise, the Further You Fall*

All good times come to an end, and Batista's high life was finally up. But fitting with his flamboyant existence, he was about to go out with a bang, one that Bloomberg News would later call the "Perfect Storm."

The first signs of financial distress came in early 2012, when Batista was actively searching for partners to team up with on various project within his holding companies. Similar to Enron finding a last-minute sucker or former Secretary Henry Paulson convincing Singapore's sovereign wealth fund to inject money into Merrill Lynch before their imminent bust, Batista searched for last-minute investors. He found them in Abu Dhabi and Germany.

He quietly negotiated with the Abu Dhabi sovereign wealth fund Mubadala to inject $2 billion for a 5.63% share in his EBX conglomerate. The investment really helped to back a valuation for EBX of about $35 billion, but only temporarily. Next, he negotiated a similar deal with German's giant utility company EON to take a stake in MBX. All this happened shortly before his entire business structure collapsed.

What initiated Batista's awkward financial position, leading him to give up more and more control of his empire, was a drama that took place at OGX, that crown jewel in the EBX holding structure.

Back in 2011, OGX claimed an early success rate in exploratory wells of more than 90%, initially valuing its oil deposits at more than $1 trillion. Even back then, there were already concerns regarding the validity of his oil reserve estimates. Large oil companies like BP and Exxon stayed well clear of Batista's business. But he had other routes to money, such as bonds, and the entrepreneur was not concerned.

Then, in 2012, further explorations and tests confirmed that the oil he had discovered was locked in a complex subsea geologic formation that made it difficult to pump out. As a result, OGX adjusted its declaration of workable sites from 90% to 87%, claiming wrongly that this high percentage of its assets would still be able to produce viable quantities of oil. This was a blatant misrepresentation of the truth, or in other words, a well-calculated lie.

Going into 2012, it became apparent that the company's wells were turning out to be duds. By the middle of 2013, the game was up. After repeatedly missing production targets, OGX publicly admitted that its wells had flopped and would be closed. In October 2013, OGX filed for bankruptcy protection after missing a $45 million interest payment on its outstanding bonds.

In November 2013, OSX filed for bankruptcy protection; soon thereafter, EBX's entire financial construct collapsed like a house of cards. With it, the foundation of Batista's wealth imploded.

Batista tried everything to save what he still believed to be the opportunity of a lifetime. He feverishly worked on restructuring plans, asset sales and mergers, but to no avail. Creditors panicked, and vultures were smelling blood. What magnified his downfall was the fact that oil prices had peaked in 2012, trading as high as $120 per barrel, only to fall to $26 a barrel by 2016. His position was further weakened by the general distrust of emerging markets, such as Brazil's, in the wake of the European financial crisis of 2011.[74]

Batista's net worth plummeted quickly. By 2012, his wealth had fallen to just $1 billion, and by 2015, he was in debt for a similar amount. His creditors were knocking on his door and, as one banker commented, he was leveraged to the hilt.

His private estate went up for grabs. One by one, he sold his most prized possessions, which included, among others, his beloved Lamborghini and other sports cars. The authorities had to speed up the liquidation procedures of Batista's estate, as rumors were flying around that he had been feverishly trying to move his remaining private reserves, such as cash and valuables, into tax havens around Latin America and Europe. In 2015, police confiscated several of his watches, a sculpture, a piano, large sums of cash, a Lamborghini, Porsche and other luxury cars in raids on two of his homes.

One of these luxury cars ended up in the private garage of the bankruptcy judge, who would later be indicted for corruption. This anecdote just highlights the deep-rooted and widespread corruption that continues to plague the South American country, both in the practices of its businesses and its opaque legal system.

Batista hit rock-bottom in January 2017, when he was arrested in a country-wide political scandal that involved the corruption of important politicians and bureaucrats. He was jailed, but was released two months later. Since then, there hasn't much news about Batista, a man who regularly covered the front pages of leading newspapers and magazines decades earlier.

## *Comparing Carlos Slim with Eike Batista*

Both similarities and differences exist between these giants of commerce and trade.

Each came from countries that have emerging economies, with all the risks, challenges, opportunities and threats such conditions bring. As individual men, both were driven by a desire for financial success. The two men possessed (and still do, even if both are slowing down) phenomenal work ethics; both were ambitious and prepared to take a gamble.

But for all the similarities, there are differences as well between the men. Perhaps for strategic reasons, perhaps because that is his personality (and probably a mixture of both), Batista craved the public eye. He wanted people to know about his flamboyance, his affairs, his wealth, his fast cars, his possessions.

The saying goes that the higher you rise, the harder you fall. That would certainly seem to be an apt description of the Brazilian entrepreneur.

By comparison, Slim is a quiet man. Fiendishly rich, fiendishly tough, fiendishly ruthless—but a man who keeps his business life and his personal life separate. As ostentatious as Batista is, then Slim is the opposite, living a relatively quiet life, enjoying the good things that money can bring, but privately. A man who is able to keep on gathering wealth, relatively speaking, out of the public eye.

We can draw lessons from the personalities of both men. Financial success, it would seem, requires bravery, a good eye for a gamble, a bit of luck, good connections and personal genius. Budding financial kings and queens can set about acquiring these characteristics; even if personal genius is hard to find within oneself, both Batista and Slim demonstrated that it can be learned from others, such as Slim's fascination with John Paul Getty.

But alongside that, we can perhaps learn that success is best sustained when our focus is on our work, not our reputation. That grows as a result of our actions, not our self-publicizing.

The two men also used different approaches to their financial work. For Slim, safe and solid was the key, building an empire from the ground up, ensuring that foundations are there to withstand the buffeting of his own decision-making and, perhaps even more importantly, the stresses that are caused by factors outside of his control, such as the recent global banking crisis.

For Batista, life was always much more of a gamble. Quick gains were what drove him on, often on the back of money that was not his—investments funded by others. It seems definitely to be the case that some risk taking is necessary in our financial lives if we wish to maximize our resources. But more importantly, the lesson from Slim is that there needs to be a framework that can cope when those gambles fail to pay off.

Slim was prepared to bet big, but only when he needed to and the odds where in his favor. While he was shuffling his chips, click, click—click click, Batista was pushing his pile to the center of the table, waiting on the draw of the card. When such a gamble pays off, the rewards are enormous, but every gambler loses in the end.

Slim has become the elder statesman, wise, sought after for his advice and well-respected beyond his native borders of Mexico. Batista, at age 61, was also destined to be on a similar path, but he was like Icarus who flew too close to the sun, burning his wings and falling back to earth. In the end, his life was a mirage. As one Brazilian twitter follower remarked both with fascination and disgust: "What did you expect?! Even his hair isn't real."[75]

## Chapter 5
# RUSSIAN OLIGARCHS

The term oligarch derives from the Greek and translates approximately as "rule by the few." It is an apt term for the Russian business elite who have emerged from the privatization of that East European economy to join the ranks of the wealthiest men on the planet. Many are close associates of Vladimir Putin, and control great swathes of Russian industry and business interests. When the dissolution of the Soviet Union occurred in the early 1990s, the void left by the state had to be filled. The oligarchs are the businessmen (rarely, if ever, women) who accumulated the massive fortunes on offer.

Who hasn't heard of Roman Abramovich, the owner of the English Premier League's Chelsea F.C? Once Britain's wealthiest man, he is now the richest citizen of Israel after being denied a renewal of his British visa. Or exiled Mikhail Khodorkovsky, once the richest man of Russia (17th on the Forbes ranking) who spent almost 10 years behind bars for openly challenging Vladimir Putin, the President of Russia. He proved that, while being part of Putin's close circle is advantageous when it comes to achieving oligarch status, it is not a prerequisite.

The stories of former KGB politburo bosses, links to the Russian Mafia, and beautiful women who have legs longer than the eye can see—it all just brings out those fuzzy feelings that could stem right out of a James Bond spy movie. One (un-named) oligarch, who sends his children to an exclusive British school arrived, for security reasons, in a fleet of black Range Rovers, most of them decoys against security threats. Security agents wait on the school grounds in case of trouble, and accompany school trips, merging into the background of whatever treat the children are enjoying.

The oligarchs live in a very strange, cloistered world. Mostly.

But it's not all private jets and expensive cars, some mundane business dealings and political chess games that require foresight and fortitude can make up daily life. Besides, not all oligarchs are created equal, and are sometimes dependent on the whims of fate that are out of their control. Let's dive into the fascinating world of money, power and vodka as we look at the lives of two Russian oligarchs, their businesses and their investment affairs.

## Mikhail Prokhorov—The Sly Fox

*"The government in Russia does not tell me what to do with my assets."*—Mikhail Prokhorov

You might know Mikhail Prokhorov as the owner of the Brooklyn Nets or as a Russian politician. This is a man with a billionaire lifestyle, jets and yachts and several giant mansions dotted around the globe. Today, he is estimated to be worth over $11 billion according to Bloomberg.76 What you may not know is his comet-like rise from simple Soviet banker to a career of savvy business management. Or how a sudden stroke of seemingly bad luck appeared to drive him into obscurity, before he shot back to fame as a rich Russian oligarch and a celebrity in the West. In his case, a scandal involving a private jet, some Russian models and a corporate power struggle ended up earning him the single biggest payday of his life—a payday in the order of billions of dollars—in cash.

### Upbringing and Career

Prokhorov was born into a middle-class Russian family; his maternal grandmother was a prominent Jewish microbiologist who had remained in Moscow during World War II to make vaccines, while his paternal grandparents were relatively wealthy peasant farmers (known as kulaks) who had suffered terrible persecution under the Soviets.

Mikhail's father, Dmitri Prokhorov, one of eight children, grew up poor in Siberia, but managed to train as a lawyer. He worked up the ranks within the Soviet Committee of Physical Culture and Sport, dealing with international relations. Unusual for a Soviet citizen, Dmitri Prokhorov had the opportunity to travel abroad and see the Western world—its riches and madness—with his own eyes. His father's tales of Western capitalism and decadence deeply impressed young Prokhorov, who began buying cheap jeans for $3 and selling them at $12 apiece when he was a teenager. He decided to study economics and finance, graduating in 1989 from the Moscow Finance Institute.

After graduation, he started a career in banking; by 1992, at the tender age of 29, he was President of the United Export-Import Bank (also known as Onetime Bank). More remarkably, he achieved all this without being a beneficiary of the Soviet Union's notoriously corrupt patronage network. He represented a new wave of educated, sophisticated businessmen, similar to the business elite in the West.

It was at Onexim Bank that he met Vladimir Potanin. Potanin, himself only 33, quickly recognized the raw talent and business acumen in Mikhail. Potanin had spent the previous 10 years working in the Soviet Union's Ministry of Foreign Trade, where he cultivated many valuable contacts within the body politic. Together with Potanin's government connections and Prokhorov's business acuity, they set out to transform the face of Russian business. As the Soviet Union collapsed and anarchy grew, they seized opportunities as they appeared, and had soon amassed significant fortunes.

## *Opportunity*

During the largely unregulated privatization of former state-controlled industries after the collapse of the Soviet Union in 1991, the new Russian government was desperately strapped for cash. In an attempt to raise funds, it sold majority stakes in some of its biggest nationalized companies. In these highly dubious auctions, state assets were acquired at extremely low prices by a small number of Russian bank consortia made up of renegades, former spies and the remaining Soviet elite. It was the dawn of a new financial hierarchy in Moscow—led by the Russian oligarchs.

This was the new reality Mikhail and Potanin had been waiting for. They studied the early process of the first auctions carefully, seeing the new Russian market's economy in action. Thanks to Potanin's Kremlin contacts, they were able to identify the most valuable assets the new government intended to sell—many of these lay in the field of precious metal mining companies.

In 1995, their moment arrived. The Russian government

announced that it was auctioning off its most valuable state-owned asset: a mining conglomerate called Norilsk Nickel. Despite producing a quarter of the world's nickel and having a turnover of over $400 million annually, Norilsk Nickel was losing cash at an alarming rate. This deterred most potential bidders. What Prokhorov and Potanin noticed, though, was that there was no reason for this, and with fresh capital and reforms, Norilsk Nickel could be made profitable—especially considering the company's vast untapped mining rights. So they devised an elaborate plan to tweak the odds to assure them success in this high-stakes poker game.

First, they made sure that Prokhorov's Onexim Bank was chosen to administer the auction, with Prokhorov himself in charge to collect bids for the government to evaluate. Potanin's newly-founded holdings company, Interros, soon established itself as a leader in the bid for ownership of Norilsk Nickel.

In fact, it was not only the leader in the bidding war, but one that was virtually unopposed. To everybody's surprise, there was only one other bid—but at $355 million, it was $184.9 million more than Interros'. As we might guess, neither of the future oligarchs would let something as minor as a higher offer get in the way of their dreams. Prokhorov simply canceled Rossiiski Kredit's bid, on the grounds that it would violate official credit limits (even though Interros' bid would violate these same limits). In the end, Prokhorov and Potanin's group won at a price that was just $100,000 higher than the reserve price of $170 million. In short, the entire auction process was a pure farce, and everyone involved knew it.[77]

Norilsk Nickel, even at a bargain basement price, was still a calculated risk for investors. It came at a substantial risk for any buyer. In 1995, the company was deeply indebted, bleeding cash at a rate of about $2 million a day due to falling nickel prices and outmoded organizational structures. Corruption and poor practice ran through the company, which leaked cash through the rusty holes in its framework.

Prokhorov rose to the challenge. In short order, he demonstrated why Potanin had chosen him as a business partner. Under his direction, the company sold off all non-core assets and regained the trust of the mining workforce by modernized equipment and improving safety.

Crucially, Prokhorov began to utilize the company's untapped mining rights. Prokhorov worked like a junior Wall Street banker, seven days a week. As a result, his company saw expansion at an impressive pace. Under his leadership, annual profits at Norilsk Nickel grew from a negative figure in 1995 to over $10 billion in 2007.[78] This time, it was rising Nickel prices that ultimately rubber-stamped the success of the company, and Prokhorov was ready to ride all the way up to the top of the Russian business world.

With the bases secured and the business flourishing, Prokhorov initiated the next phase of Norilsk Nickel's growth path. He completely revamped and modernized the company to prepare it for the international competition it now faced. He even took personal charge to drastically improve environmental policies within his company.

But his environmentally-sound maneuvers were not made out of pure charity or any higher calling to bring Russia back to old glories. Being a fervent student of modern capitalism, he made sure that he would be generously compensated for his work. Along the way, he accumulated an equity position through preferred shares and stock options, eventually making him the second-largest shareholder after Potanin.[79] Not too bad for an ordinary middle-class person without prior political pedigree and virtually no former wealth in a country that permitted very little social mobility.

When the company went public after their privatization was completed in September 2004, it was payday. Prokhorov and Potanin instantly became multi-billionaires. But that wasn't the end of Prokhorov's rocketing rise. This is where we finally meet the femmes fatales of this tale—a bevy of beautiful Russian models that suggested a playboy lifestyle, allied to his fondness for hanging out on his private jets. With the Russian oligarch, though, it was more work hard, play hard. In the end, those women would play their part in helping Prokhorov to secure his wealth and at the same time, make him the more mature person that he is today. But he had a complex and convoluted path to follow to end up at this destination.[80]

### *The Courchevel Incident*

In January 2007, on a typically icy Russian winter morning, it was time to celebrate the Russian Orthodox New Year. Mikhail Prokhorov and a group of close friends boarded his private jet to an upscale French ski resort called Courchevel. With them were eight aspiring models from an agency managed by some of his business associates. Everything was fine until three days in, when a heavily-armed squad of 50 riot policemen stormed the private resort Prokhorov and his party occupied. The dream vacation came to a sudden end.

What had happened? A terrorist threat, or a simple mistake by local law enforcement?

Rumors were rife that the women were high-class prostitutes (though there's no evidence the women were anything more than models) and that the Russian Mafiosi were present. Stories of drunken saunas, hot baths (in more ways than just the water temperature) and snow angels abounded. If this were not bad enough, tales began to emerge of naked men and women prancing around, singing in the snow. But Courchevel is best known as a wealthy, but family-orientated, resort. Yes, the designer sunglasses and snowboards might proliferate, but so do the children's classes filled with would-be skiers. The reputation of the resort was at stake. Something had to be done!

The truth of the matter was, in some ways, much more mundane, although the consequences for Prokhorov were not. A very peculiar string of coincidences revealed a power struggle among the greatest Russian oligarchs that ended with Prokhorov losing all control of the company he had built up—Norilsk Nickel.

### The Truth Behind the Outrage

What really happened? Les Trois Vallées, in the French and Swiss Alps, has always been a popular spot for Russians with money. Since the fall of the Iron Curtain, the nouveau riche and the remaining Russian political elite would frequently spend their winter vacation there, drinking champagne and the best Glühwein, and enjoying the good Western life. But in 2004, the area was particularly flooded with Russian tourists, and Prokhorov was just one of many guests in that upscale ski resort of Courchevel.

What he couldn't have known at that time was that the among these many Russians vacationers were a few that were on the top of the list of criminals wanted by both Interpol and the French police. During the months of December 2003 and January 2004, an extensive police investigation was in full throttle, searching and hunting down the infamous Russian mafia, with its drug, weapons and human trafficking dealers.

At that time, the French police had already searched several hotels but didn't find anything suspicious, until, the story goes, an anonymous tipster handed in an old Russian newspaper article from a local Russian gossip paper, the kind most countries endure, but which none but the most gullible take seriously.

The original articles focused on a friend of Prokhorov, Hloponin, a politician and businessman. The story was riddled with speculation and rumor; at times it was pure fiction. It made allegations about Russian oligarchs and a supposed collection of call girls with whom they liked to associate. Assertions were made regarding a mythical "French elite procurer Romeo."[81] The French police put two and together and made five. The article, alongside the rumors of what was going on in Courchevel, were enough to prompt the police raid. If they hoped to find Hloponin among the life-loving party, they would be unlucky. He was not a frequent visitor to Courchevel. But the investigation was also seeking evidence of corrupt practices, and linked the goings-on in Courchevel with these.

Even though the French police couldn't understand the intricate relationship between the competing Russian factions, it was the missing clue that would identify the crimes they feared were taking place. Some background research had soon connected Prokhorov. The fact that he even took "models" with him underlined the general suspicion of Prokhorov being a pimp, and who know what else.

On the morning of the raid, Prokhorov and his entire entourage were arrested on charges of sexual facilitation (or pimping) and solicitation. The girls were released immediately, along with his friends, but Prokhorov had to extend his stay in France for a reason he had no wish to pursue. He spent four full days in custody until he was eventually released and all charges were dropped. But the damage was done. To this day, Prokhorov hasn't returned to Courchevel, and to this day, he demands an official apology from French police authorities. As we shall see, he had good reasons to be outraged.

### Forced to Sell—But with a Happy Ending

Back in Moscow, the scandal-hungry boulevard press made the most of Prokhorov's arrest story. Prokhorov found himself constantly on the front page of the spicier magazines, which ridiculed his arrest as both a "pimp" and a mastermind criminal—they were unsure about which to be most outraged. Through their articles, these publications seized the opportunity to question his character and leadership skills. In short, the period marked a complete PR disaster for both himself and Norilsk Nickel. It couldn't have come at a more inopportune time.

Unbeknownst to the public, before Prokhorov left for his rather indecent vacation escapade in France, he and Potanin were in heated disagreement over the business strategy of Norilsk Nickel. Both Prokhorov and Potanin were at odds and a stalemate loomed, threatening a long-lasting and complicated corporate struggle at the top—Russian style. Prokhorov's arrest in France and the associated embarrassment for him (and, therefore, his company) changed all this.

With Prokhorov against the wall, and in light of the scandal, he had no choice other than to resign from Norilsk Nickel's board and give up all his functions as an executive. Potanin, his long-term partner and early mentor, convinced the board to let Prokhorov go. To add the alcohol of shame to the fire, Potanin offered to buy out Prokhorov at an absurdly discounted price.[82] The deal would mark Potanin's total victory and Prokhorov's complete embarrassment. But the oligarch had underestimated Prokhorov's resolve and cunning. His former friend would shortly serve a decisive blow to Potanin, the likes of which he is still dealing with to this day.

One cannot ignore the distinct suspicion of a brazen set-up that trapped Prokhorov in Courchevel. Such Machiavellian strategies might seem like the stuff of mindless Hollywood films, but there is a hint of truth about their existence. The anonymous tipster who gave the police the information that led to Prokhorov's arrest had serious consequences and someone would sure profit back in Moscow. Yet at least Prokhorov's reaction can raise no doubt of these same suspicions. At the beginning of 2008, Prokhorov turned for help to another powerful oligarch, who would work as a white knight and bail him out of his problems, paying a fair market price for the privilege.

The other oligarch in question was no other than Oleg Deripaska, who in 2007 was top-dog among Russian oligarchs. In control of United Company RUSAL, another mining conglomerate, his net worth was estimated to be $28 billion. He was by far the richest and most powerful oligarch, one with very close ties to the Kremlin and Putin himself. Like his peers, he had shown an uncanny ruthlessness in growing RUSAL to become the top mining company in Russia, and, at the same time, propelling himself to the top of the pecking order of oligarchs.

For Deripaska, Norilsk Nickel was the perfect strategic fit to integrate into his growing commercial and mining empire. Something he could achieve, crucially, with the blessing of the Russian hierarchy.

By April of 2008, Prokhorov had officially transferred his 25% stake in Norilsk Nickel to Oleg Deripaska, in exchange for some 14% of RUSAL stock and cash—lots of it. The same month, about $5 billion hit Prokhorov's personal bank account, with another tranche of $2 billion expected to be transferred later that year.

In total, Prokhorov looked like he was ending up with over $7 billion in cash and RUSAL stock worth another $3 billion. The takeover battle was officially over, with Deripaska as the winner—or so he thought. In any case, Potanin would have to struggle with a new owner and director at the top of Norisk Nickel, someone with staying power and very deep pockets. With Potanin controlling 30% of Norilsk and Deripaska controlling 27.8%, years of legal battle to decide the supremacy at the top of Norisk Nickel then ensued. This was much to the amusement of other oligarchs and the Moscow elite. The stalemate that Potanin wanted to avoid, and thought he achieved by ousting Prokhorov, was now much more engrained. Meanwhile, Prokhorov was out of this particular game—with all his money—and some more—intact.

As awful as it might have seemed back during that winter in Courchevel, the events then had been serendipitous. Prokhorov's fortune was greater than ever.

In September 2008, only a few months after the point when billions of dollars' worth of cash hit Prokhorov's private account, a confused and cornered US investment bank was about to bring havoc not only to the US markets, but also to the global financial system. The impacts of the subprime collapse had devastating effects on the wealth of many oligarchs in Russia, but not Prokhorov.

Global financial markets went into a tailspin as Lehman Brothers announced their bankruptcy. Liquidity dried up around the world, a full-blown panic broke out and all asset classes, including commodities, plummeted like rocks. With them, they dragged down many aspiring oligarchs, including two of the once richest men in Russia: Oleg Deripaska and Potanin. How lucky Prokhorov had been to get out of Norilsk Nickel when he did, even if the decision to do so had been forced upon him.

By early 2009, Oleg Deripaska's net worth plunged 85%, from $28 billion to a low of $4 billion in less than year. Still a fortune almost the entire remainder of the world's population can only dream about, but a seven-times fall in wealth. With Prokhorov's $5 billion in cash in his bank account, and more to come soon, Mikhail Prokhorov found himself at the top of the Forbes list of richest men in Russia, with an estimated $9.5 billion. The big difference with most of his peers, of course, was that he had almost 70% of his wealth in liquid assets, such as cash and short-term bonds, instead of plummeting stocks. With prices depressed around the world, Prokhorov was like a child in a candy shop, with pockets filled with cash. It was time to go shopping, but perhaps not to the stores you would expect.

## *Back of the Nets—A Sporting Purchase*

On September 24, 2009, it was announced that an unknown Russian billionaire would rescue the New Jersey Nets. That unnamed man was Mikhail Prokhorov. At the age of 44, Prokhorov was about to become not only the first Russian, but first non-American, to own and control an NBA basketball team. Himself an avid basketball fan and player (he is 6'6" tall), he said in a statement, "I have a long-standing passion for basketball and pursuing interests that forward the development of the sport in Russia." Furthermore, he made the claim at his initial press conference in 2010 that: "the Nets would win a championship within five years."

For many fans and basketball experts, a sense of pure astonishment descended as an unknown foreigner had bought a team that was ridiculed as one of the worst in the NBA, and that obviously was in financial trouble. Hence, Prokhorov was celebrated as the "Russian white knight," although many experts openly speculated whether Prokhorov knew what he was doing and whether he was buying nothing more than a dud. The New York Times headlined a news article as "Richest Russian's Newest Toy: An N.B.A. Team."[83] And the Business Insider commented, with a sense of doom, "We'll see."[84] In retrospect, we can see that they both underestimated Prokhorov's business acumen and understanding of opportunity and value.

For Prokhorov, it wasn't only his passion for basketball that put a big smile on his face during the official press conferences. On his personal blog, he wrote of the deal as a "very profitable business project." At that time, neither the NBA nor financial experts agreed with him, but Prokhorov knew better.

Under the terms of the deal, Prokhorov paid $200 million for an 80% share in the ownership of the team, holding the option to purchase the remainder later from then owner Bruce C. Ratner, a well-known New York real estate developer.[85] What many overlooked in the hype that surrounded the idea of a foreigner owning an NBA team was Prokhorov's much larger financial commitment to purchase a 45% interest in the new arena that Ratner was planning for the Nets in Brooklyn.

The arena was meant to be the centerpiece of a 22-acre, $4.9 billion development project known as Atlantic Yards, and located at Atlantic and Flatbush Avenues in the heart of Brooklyn. It should have become Ratner's lifetime achievement, bringing him fame and eternal recognition among his peers in New York City. Unfortunately, he was running out of funds, and he himself was in dire financial condition due to the aftermath of the subprime crisis. Prokhorov's cash injection was more than welcome. As a matter of fact, so welcome that Prokhorov got the right to purchase up to 20% of the Atlantic Yards Development Company that Ratner controlled, and which would develop the non-arena real estate in the project.

All went according to plan. In May 2010, the NBA gave its official seal of approval, with the blessing of Michael Bloomberg, then major of New York City. In December 2015, Prokhorov purchased the remaining 20% of the Nets and the remaining 55% of the Arena from Ratner. This valued the team and arena at a combined $1.7 billion. According to sources, $400 million would flow in this final transaction from Prokhorov directly to Ratner's pockets. Not too shabby for an initial investment of $200 million. But it gets better.

In April 2018, the NBA officially announced that Joe Tsai, e-commerce giant, co-founder and chairman of Alibaba Group, had purchased 49% of the Nets from Prokhorov with the option to purchase more shares in 2021 and take over the controlling interest in the team.[86] According to the New York Post, this deal would eventually value the Nets at $2.35 billion. The timing of the sale couldn't have been better. The Nets are the second-highest valued company in the NBA, in return for very mediocre sports performances. Many experts today see this as an excessive valuation for a sports franchise.[87]

As timely as his sale might be, Prokhorov still controls 51% of the Nets, which he will most likely sell at an even higher price further down the road (but still within the next three years). And here comes the best part: The deal does not include the ownership of the renamed Barclays Center.[88] Prokhorov still owns every bit of that and anyone who knows Brooklyn's real estate market today can imagine that Prokhorov is sitting on a fine fortune, generating plenty of rental income each month. [89] And that's something of an understatement.

## Oleg Deripaska—The Russian Bear

*"There is no one in Russia whom I can't reach in less than one hour."—Oleg Deripaska*

Oleg Vladimirovich Deripaska: Russian and Cyprus businessman, billionaire, bookworm and physicist, aluminum tycoon and close Putin confident.

He was ranked ninth on the list of the world's richest people in 2008, according to Forbes magazine. He was once the richest person in Russia with a net worth estimated to be $28 billion. How he achieved this, at what speed, and all at such a young age is even more impressive.

You could see him travel in one of his private Gulfstream Aerospace aircraft, leading a jetsetter life. Attending conferences around the world and making friends among the global elite, at places such as Davos during the World Economic Forum, or the US in New York and Washington. He could not have known that these would, one day, be his downfall.

His unprecedented rise in the new Russian hierarchy was followed by an equally rapid downfall, one that saw him being personally humiliated on national TV by no other than Putin himself. Although a lengthy recovery and gradually getting back into grace with Putin saw a return to old glories, he seemed to lose it all again—and this time for good.

### Upbringing and Career

Deripaska was born on January 2 in 1968 in Dzershinsk, a city in

Nizhniy Novgorod Oblast, in the former Soviet Russia. And although born in the city 400 kilometers (250 miles) east of Moscow, he grew up in Ust-Labinsk, Krasnodar Krai on his grandfather's small farm.

His parents divorced when he was a toddler, and at the age of 4 he moved to the Krasnodar region in southern Russia to live with his mother's parents until they passed away. He continued living with his paternal grandparents from the age of eight. His father, a military engineer, died when he was 12.

Raised in a small rural settlement where he rode horses and tended chickens, pigs and cows, Deripaska says his grandparents imbued him with the notion that one had to live off the land to survive.[90] His grandfather always told him, "If you want to eat—work!" To this day, he is proud of his rural background and love for nature. He once said: "I don't like Moscow. It's not my city."

During his upbringing, he gained a passion for reading that continues to this day. He was always an outstanding student and finished school with excellent grades. His teachers and former classmates say that he was always at the top when it came to math, chemistry or physics. His talent for these helped him to enroll at the Physics department of Moscow State University in 1985.

After a year at the university, he was conscripted into the armed forces and served in the Soviet army's Strategic Missile Forces in the Trans-Baikal area in Siberia. He served three years there before he returned to the university. In interviews, he still speaks fondly of his experiences: "I was in charge of security at a very big complex," he says. "I learned how to manage people in the army."

When he returned to the university in 1988, he completed his physics degree, adopting his grandfather's dictum by working nights and summers, doing construction jobs to make ends meet.[91] He had big dreams of becoming a theoretical physicist but with the fall of the Soviet Union and without funding, Deripaska had to look for alternatives—and he found one!

### *A Rising Star*

In 1991, when the Soviet Union collapsed, he made his first steps as a businessman. He teamed up with friends from the university and together they founded VTK, a metals trading company. Deripaska, though, took overall charge. Taking advantage of the ensuing chaos after the collapse of the Soviet Union, he adopted a systematic, scientific approach to commodity trading and buying and selling raw materials.

The business was simple. Deripaska undertook export arbitrage, buying metals and raw materials at low Russian prices and selling them abroad at much higher international market prices, hence making hard currency income. With a clever infrastructure that had offices in the Baltic States, he was able to shelter his profits from any taxes. His boldness and drive to succeed paid off quickly. He made his first million dollars on his second transaction.[92]

### *Networking, Russian-Style*

With his financial success, he had tasted blood and he wanted more. But he was motivated by more than simply earning money quickly. He avoided wasting the finances earned through trading, unlike like so many of his compatriots, who spent it to provide instant, but short-lived, gratification. Within the chaos of the collapse of the Soviet Union, he clearly understood the once-in-a-lifetime opportunity that was offered to him. He had bigger dreams and for that, he needed every ruble and dollar he could muster.

He decided to invest his new-found wealth. This enabled him to expand his business reach and to make use of the vast opportunities that were still lying ahead of him. But he also understood that time was of the essence. Unfortunately, being as young as Deripaska was just after graduation, without any political cache, business contacts or experience, his horizons were limited.

He needed more than just his raw talents and youthful drive. He needed the right contacts and he needed guidance; he needed access to important business networks and, most importantly, capital. He found it in Michael and Lev Cherney, Jewish Ukraine-born brothers and entrepreneurs with a background of knowing how to intimidate other business people.

The Cherneys owned Trans World Group (TWG), which had become the most powerful industrial holding company in Russia following the collapse of the Soviet Union. Lev was an official business leader in Russia, and Michael was responsible for acquaintances, especially relationships with government officials.

Deripaska met Michael Cherney at the Metals Bulletin conference in London. The meeting proved to be very fruitful for both of them, and Cherney decided to take Deripaska under his wing. Michael was looking for talented managers for his rapidly expanding aluminum empire. He was especially looking for someone who could oversee the smelting and production process, a job that required drive, endurance and the somewhat Russian resilience to deal with cold winters.

Deripaska didn't disappoint. He worked eagerly to do Michael's bidding. In return, Michael showed him the good life. Dinners in Paris, flights in private jets, and introductions to the elite of industry and politics in Moscow.

Deripaska learned fast, absorbed everything and in the process, got increasingly more ambitious. He understood that only through business ownership could he attain the reach and influence he required to realize his grand vision—to change and modernize Russia. His opportunity to own such a business would soon come.

In 1992, Russia began privatizing state enterprises by handing out shares to employees and distributing vouchers that could be converted into stock.

Deripaska decided to invest his own money in Sayanogorsk, a smelter in southern Siberia. He bought up all the shares and vouchers he could lay his hands on. For that, he used all his arbitrage and trading profits to buy his initial stake in this smelter. In the process, he accumulated a 20% stake in the factory, making him the biggest individual shareholder (after the state itself).

To finalize his control over Sayanogorsk, Deripaska asked Michael Cherney for financial and strategic support. The Cherney brothers invested in Sayanogorsk alongside Deripaska, giving their student control over the Sayanogorsk plant. In the process, he quickly made himself the director general and chairman. It was 1994 and Deripaska had just passed his 26th birthday. His star was on the rise.

### *Aluminum Wars*

Deripaska kept this position at the Sayanogorsk smelter until it was merged and integrated into a new holding company, called the Sibirsky Aluminum Group, in 1997, which was jointly controlled and owned by Deripaska and Michael Cherney. Deripaska led this newly-formed group as president, transforming it into a conglomerate with a wide variety of business interests in Russia.

During this period, he matured as a manager and leader. He made sure that he read and learned everything there was to know about aluminum production, and in the process formulated his own management and leadership style. Deripaska became a follower of the kaizen-Japanese concept of success, which is based on continuous development and effective production processes.

Early on, he was convinced that management needed to be undertaken from the front, like a real military leader would do. He believed that one needed to have a hands-on approach to be successful in the rough, tough world of an industry in dire need of strong leadership. And in this business, a leader had to know about the production just as much as the administrator back in Moscow. In doing so, he would also gain the respect and loyalty of his plant workers.

Enduring the long, harsh Siberian winters could sap the will and loyalty of even the toughest of hardy Russian workers. But the example he set ensured that he maintained his workforce's loyalty. He would need that commitment, as during the same period, violence broke out among competing factions of the aluminum industry. The conflicts saw many of his fellow aluminum managers killed. The period is today recorded in history as the time of the "aluminum wars."

The aluminum-producing industry had once been united under the centralized leadership of the Soviet Union in Moscow. But soon after the collapse of Communism, the industry splintered into many factions, and independent smelters spread all over the Siberian Arctic Circle. Each smelter was ruled by its own local "warlord," who controlled his own army of workers.

It was clear to everyone involved that the industry needed leadership and, most importantly, law and order. Consolidating the various smelters was the only sensible solution, but it needed someone with more than just financial genius and political contacts. Drive and determination, alongside physical and emotional bravery, were key requisites of whomever took on this role of consolidation. Deripaska was that man.

Unfortunately, not everyone in Russia shared the drive and ambition of young Deripaska. Seeing the young upstart promoted was a personal humiliation for many former Communist-era plant bosses. On top of that, many officials in Moscow and Siberia disliked the increasing tentacles of the Cherney brothers. With aggressive tax evasion and heavy-hand tactics that bordered on

Mafia-style intimidation and violence, the brothers developed an increasingly bad reputation that forged powerful enemies within Moscow, as well as in Siberia. It would only be a matter of time until someone would challenge the ambitious trio of the Cherney brothers and Deripaska.

And so, they did! As Deripaska was consolidating his hold on Sayanogorsk, gun battles were breaking out across Siberia aluminum smelters. In interviews, Deripaska described that period as "anarchy." According to a widely-told story, Deripaska and his entourage were attacked at Sayanogorsk with a grenade launcher and were forced to camp out in the smelter to protect it from an armed takeover.[93]

In these skirmishes, he lost two of his senior managers at an aluminum plant that was vied for by a competing faction. In retaliation, he admitted in an interview with The Financial Times, he "destroyed" the group that had attacked him. Out of these aluminum wars, Deripaska emerged as the clear winner.

## *RUSAL—The Beginning*

The violence didn't do much to halt Deripaska's drive to get more aluminum smelters under his control. Together with the Cherney brothers, Deripaska controlled almost half of the Russian aluminum production capacity by early 2000.[94]

It came to a showdown that year between the two last remaining factions of aluminum production. On the one side were Deripaska and the Cherney brothers, and on the other stood another powerful oligarch—Roman Abramovich.

Abramovich was a resourceful and determined opponent. He had both financial and political cache. He accumulated his aluminum portfolio through Sibneft, the state-owned oil company, which he had controlled for four years since the fall of the Soviet Union. In Moscow, he was well-connected. It was said that he enjoyed the approval of the newly appointed President, Vladimir Putin.

The meeting that took place on February 17, 2000 would be decisive for all parties involved. Nothing less than the future of Russia's industrial prowess was at stake: a prowess to create a national champion that would be able to compete in international markets.

And so, in a mood of conciliation and patriotic fervor, both parties came to an agreement. It was decided that Deripaska's collection of producers would work alongside Sibneft, controlled by Roman Abramovich, in a merger. The new company formed by the merger would be named Russian Aluminum, or RUSAL, in which Sibal (Deripaska's firm) and Sibneft each had a 50% stake. Together the new entity would control close to 90% of Russia's aluminum industry. [95]

The biggest surprise in this deal was that the new entity would be led by Oleg Deripaska, who had just turned 32 at the time. He was appointed to run the company as its general manager, while Abramovich would step back from operations but remain a majority shareholder.[96]

On his side, Abramovich, as one of the richest of Russians, was looking for new challenges—among them living abroad and owning a Premier League soccer team. It seemed he had had enough of Russian industrial and political power games. Deripaska, on the other hand, was on his way up to reaching the pinnacle of success. Abramovich had been there and was happy to be on the way out.

In 2007, Deripaska took the last independent competitor in the Russian aluminum market under his control, crowning his achievements by merging RUSAL with Russian aluminum rival OAO Sual Group and the alumina assets of Glencore. In the process, RUSAL became the world's biggest aluminum producer.[97]

In just three years of managing this newly-formed entity, Deripaska shaped RUSAL into an aluminum empire that would reach the top ten in world producers of aluminum. To gain full control over RUSAL, Deripaska gradually bought out Abramovich's stake over the following years.

Deripaska achieved his dream of unifying all aluminum producers in Russia, reinventing the industry that existed during the Soviet era. Through the industry, he created a national champion that was able to compete with the elites of the world and in return, receive the respect it always deserved.

### *First Fall*

As his empire grew, so did Deripaska's personal wealth. By 2008, he became the richest person in Russia, with an estimated net worth of $23 billion, and he was ninth in the world's ranking of the super-rich. But his explosive rise came at a cost—a string of unfortunate events was about to, almost, bring him to his knees and create a struggle for financial survival in years to come.

His ambitions did not stop at being Russia's richest man. He had even bigger dreams that went beyond just aluminum production. With Siberian Aluminum functioning as the core holding company, Deripaska went on an unprecedented shopping spree. He transformed the company into a vehicle of acquisition that would later look like a Russian doll, containing one company within another.

He renamed Siberian Aluminum to Basic Elements in 2001. The new company held a wide interest in various industrial and commercial assets. But at its core was another company called EN+ Group. And within EN+ Group was Deripaska's crown jewel: RUSAL.

Established in 2006, EN+ Group combined all mining, metals and energy interests within Basic Elements group. Deripaska had special plans for EN+ Group. He wanted it to become a full-service resources company, similar to BHP or Rio Tinto. In 2008, he got the chance to move one step further along the road towards realizing his vision.

Earlier that year, Mikhail Prokhorov, the dandy oligarch who was charged with pimping in France in the winter of 2007, came knocking on Deripaska's doors to get help to solve a dispute between him and Potanin, his long-time business partner and fellow oligarch.

Deripaska saw a perfect opportunity. Norris Nickel was widely regarded as one of Russia's most valuable companies, with vast untapped resources. In April 2008, he took over Prokhorov's 25% stake in Norris Nickel at market price, making him instantly the second-largest shareholder for cash and shares in RUSAL. With this investment, he would not only be the world's leading producer of aluminum, but also industrial-grade nickel and palladium production. But from there on, everything came crushing down on Deripaska and his complex empire of assets and business interests.

September 2008 marked the culmination point of the subprime crisis, with Lehman Brothers filing for bankruptcy. Credit markets completely dried up. A global liquidity crisis followed, forcing banks around the world to shut their doors for capital hungry debtors—which included Russian oligarchs such as Deripaska.

Things quickly turned from bad to worse as commodity prices dropped dramatically in the light of a worldwide recession.

Companies Deripaska had acquired in recent years were bleeding cash, and with crashing commodity prices, the financial losses stacked up rapidly. A syndicate of banks that had financed Deripaska's acquisitions came calling, demanding their money back. Without access to new funding, Deripaska had no choice but to default on a series of loans

Shares in RUSAL and Norilsk plunged, dropping more than 70% from April to the end of 2008. With the high prices gone, Deripaska quickly lost his status as the richest man in Russia. Instead, he found he was on the way down to the no-man's land of lower-ranked and fallen Russian entrepreneurs who had themselves been caught out by the US-inspired global crisis. But those who knew Deripaska well didn't write him off—at least not yet.

### *Rising Again*

It is said that at times of crisis, a person's true character would reveal itself. Deripaska had the chance to demonstrate impressively the character of which he was made.

Despite his dire financial situation, he confronted the challenges ahead. He created a task force that contained a dedicated location he himself would oversee. He called it the "war room"—a place where he could negotiate with creditors and vulture investors.

Working endlessly to secure new funding and to refinance his existing debt, he managed to keep his crippling empire alive. Firstly, day by day, then into weeks and months, he worked and schemed—that maxim of his grandfather once more—until he was able to see the light at the end of the tunnel. His hard work, tenaciousness and sheer willpower paid off.

In November 2008, Deripaska secured a $4.5 billion loan from state-owned Vnesheconombank, or VEB, to refinance the syndicate loan. The Russian press called it a government bailout, but the emergency funding came at a steep cost to Deripaska and his holding company. "We paid very high interest rates," Deripaska recalled, "VEB made a half a billion dollars in 18 months."

Deripaska says he never worried about the bank seizing his assets. He knew they had no interest in running RUSAL's smelters and mines, which span the globe from Siberia to Nigeria. The government had a strategic interest to see Deripaska and his mining empire survive. But this too, came at a cost—deep loyalty to the current government under the leadership of Vladimir Putin and his underling, Medvedev.

After securing the necessary funding to survive, Deripaska cut costs throughout his conglomerate. In 2009, he slashed expenditures at RUSAL by 25%. He searched everywhere for savings that could be made, from shutting smelters to changing suppliers. He gave the banks a detailed account of his moves, so that they too could understand the slow but steady progress he was making.

Some of the cost-cutting went too far; for example, at one point, his mining workers didn't get paid for weeks, until Vladimir Putin himself chose to scold Deripaska in a show of public witch-hunting that rivaled even Donald Trump's showmanship. On national TV, Putin ordered Deripaska in front of the board and the workers' unions to sign an agreement of personal liability.[98] A personal humiliation to say the least! But as degrading as it might have been, it guaranteed Deripaska's survival as a part of Putin's future plans for Russia.

By December 2009, he reached a final agreement with more than 70 Russian and foreign banks to refinance $17 billion of debt. Prokhorov agreed to swap some of his debt for a larger stake in RUSAL, and the company began lining up investors for the company's Hong Kong initial public offering. Deripaska was able to hold on to his prized asset, Norilsk, as he vied for complete control with the largest shareholder, Potanin. A fight that would last years in a London court.

In 2010, RUSAL became the first Russian company to be listed on the Hong Kong Stock Exchange. With a recovering economy that helped boost commodity prices and with the subsequent increase in share prices, Deripaska was slowly overcoming his financial crisis. With his bet on China as a future leading economy, his resource-heavy empire profited from China's rise to become the second-largest economy in the world.

In November 2014, Deripaska officially became President of RUSAL, which by this time employed more than 61,000 people in 20 countries across five continents.

In 2017, Deripaska was able to list his resource holding company EN+ on the London Stock Exchange—a crowning moment of his career and an object of prestige among his fellow Russian oligarchs! It was listed November 2017 in a $1.5 billion flotation, giving it a market capitalization of about $8 billion.[99]

He was back at the top again and all looked better than ever. It looked as if all his work and struggles for financial survival and recognition would succeed. But while he was back at the top, fate still had something else in mind. He would soon face the abyss a second time.

### *Down Again*

On Friday, April 6, 2018, the share prices of RUSAL collapsed by more than 12%. Shares prices in EN+, Deripaska's metals and resources holding company, suffered even harsher declines, falling by more than 20% until trading in EN+ was suspended by UK regulators.[100] Within weeks, shares in RUSAL trading at the Hong Kong Stock Exchange fell from year highs of HK$ 6.36 to a year low of HK$ 1.31. With these price declines, Deripaska's fortune dwindled away for a second time, and this time it seemed for good! No "war room" or even his best connections in power and influence could rescue him this time.

What happened? The steep declines were preceded by a White House announcement that the Trump administration had posed sanctions on seven high-profile Russian businessmen, 12 companies, and 17 senior Russian government officials—known as the "Kremlin's list"—who, according to Trump's presidency, were "benefiting from the Putin regime and playing a key role in advancing Russia's malign activities."[101]

Steven Mnuchin, the Treasury Secretary, commented in an official press conference: "Russian oligarchs and elites who profit from this corrupt system will no longer be insulated from the consequences of their government's destabilizing activities."

The sanctions included a freeze on any US assets held by those on the list, banning them from doing business with US citizens—in effect cutting them off from US finance, trade and investment. What magnified the impact was that sanctions would also apply to non-US citizens who, according to the US Treasury, "knowingly facilitate significant transactions, including deceptive or structured transactions, for or on behalf of any person subject to US sanctions."

As market observers commented, the announcements equaled a death sentence for international trade, especially for sellers of commodities that trade in US dollars. By far the hardest hit on that list was Deripaska.

It was the first time the US had gone after an oligarch and his entire business empire. It was understood as a clear warning to other Russian billionaires and industrialists who have cultivated close links to President Vladimir Putin. In a twist of fate, Deripaska's proximity to high-level influencers in the Kremlin, including Putin himself—the very factors that once helped him establish his empire—were now a gigantic liability to his business ambitions.

The consequences were immediate and dramatic. The Hong Kong-listed company lost a number of directors when they quit the board. Formerly loyal clients stopped trading with Deripaska almost immediately, and the prestige of being listed in London was terminated as he saw his company delisted by UK regulators.

The impact on operations had a startling effect on Deripaska's still fragile finances. Again, there were severe financial problems—deeper and more complex than ever before. In a public announcement, RUSAL warned of credit defaults and told its customers to stop paying the company after sanctions barred it from conducting any trade in US dollars or doing business with US citizens. Analysts and bankers told The Financial Times they believed the company would collapse without state support, given widespread fears among international banks that any association with the company could drag them into the US Treasury's net, rounding up its own definition of rogue enterprises.

A rescue from a friendly investor with very deep pockets was also unlikely. In the past, there had always been China to count on, especially for resource-rich countries like Russia, and those who dealt in natural resources. China had helped Russian entities operating under sanctions in the past, but this time the country had its own financial challenges to deal with, that included reforms of its credit markets and a potential trade and currency war with the US. Besides, the country was awash in aluminum production itself, and efforts were being made to reform and downsize the industry—not to expand it in Russia.

There was only one option left: to admit defeat and save what could still be rescued. Deripaska gave up control of RUSAL by reducing his majority stake in EN+. He stepped down from RUSAL, withdrawing from all official functions in May 2018. Furthermore, he cut his 70% holding in EN+ to below 50% and resigned from its board. This included EN+, thus relinquishing any rights to nominate the chief executive of RUSAL. In effect, he gave up complete control of the company he had led with enormous success and in doing so, was degraded to the role of a passive majority shareholder. The move would, in effect, sever the Russian tycoon from the aluminum empire he built from the ashes of the Soviet Union.

But his personal sacrifices and severe blows to his ego didn't stop there. In an act that can only be interpreted as one of financial desperation, it was announced that Deripaska had listed three of his private Gulfstream Aerospace jets for sale to provide liquidity for his dwindling empire. They were listed at $30 million each, a fraction of what they once were worth. With that, his jet-setting lifestyle and trips to Davos World Economic Forum seemed to have ended for the foreseeable future.

## *Comparing Mikhail Prokhorov with Oleg Deripaska*

Two billionaires, both of whom made their fortunes from the fall of the Soviet Empire. Each understood that the political upheaval offered an enormous opportunity—one that required boldness, aggression and drive to make changes and ultimately improve the state of their home country.

They are both from the same generation, but Prokhorov, we might conclude, was smarter. He cashed out at the peak of the markets and diversified away from his old business, old ties and old connections. He did not wish to become over-reliant on them. Today, he still has exposure to his initial interests in mining, but also has his prized possession in New York City.

Prokhorov freed himself from the old obsessions and complicated ties, and he evolved. Deripaska never made that final step.

Even though Prokhorov is politically active in Russia, he has kept a relative distance from the real inner power circle of the Kremlin. Deripaska didn't, and it ultimately cost him dearly.

Deripaska might have made many friends among the business and political elite in Russia and Moscow, but Prokhorov has a much more diversified base and most importantly, stays on good terms with the US. Whereas Deripaska had been having difficulties entering the United States since 1993, and now is completely prohibited from going there, Prokhorov is more of an international jet-setter rather than a rural warlord.

Both of their lives have been marked with battles, tough fights, high risks and high stakes. But whereas Prokhorov has radically transformed himself after selling Norisk Nickel, settling into a (relatively) quieter life, Deripaska has continued to fight.

While that might be a more heroic and honorable fight in the eyes of an-old fashioned bear, Deripaska spread himself too thinly. No one can deny that Prokhorov has always picked his battles, but he understood when to withdraw and when to stand up and be counted.

Deripaska was, and will remain, the Russian bear he so resembles. Brave, defiant, powerful, and loyal, but ultimately facing the threat of extinction. By contrast, Prokhorov is a cautious and cunning fox, surviving on his wits and living well as a result. It also has to be said that luck shone on him.

Both one-time rich and powerful men, but there is no doubt as to who is currently the more successful of the two.

Today, Prokhorov's personal wealth is estimated to be $11 billion, ranking him comfortably in the top 100 wealthiest people in the world. His interests range from mining operations to sports franchises and real estate. He has become his own family office, managing his own assets. His liquid wealth has given him all the options he needs and the lifestyle of which he has always dreamed.

He might not be the richest or most powerful oligarch any more, but that was never his ambition. He still knows how to make a buck or two. He always understood how to make money in Russia, so why not in America as well? He might have been extremely lucky with the circumstances surrounding the sale of his Norilsk Nickel interests in 2008, but he has always possessed the DNA of a shrewd business operator, owner and tactician, alongside the immeasurable benefit of a good hand for timing.

Certainly, he had his rough years, confirming all the stereotypes of a young Russian billionaire. But he changed. It seems that after the traumatic events of 2007 and his short time in prison, his power struggle with one of today's most powerful Russian oligarchs, and his relationship with another, Prokhorov changed as a person and businessman. Both for the better.

Today, he is a philanthropist and a reputable Russian politician, one who has surprisingly good standing with the US government. He comes over as reasoned, more of an elder statesman than his age would suggest. A man who understands when to take his spot in the limelight and when not to. Most importantly, he knows how to complete deals.

For example, while he was negotiating a lucrative deal with Tsai, several US federal prosecutors and powerful US government organizations were preparing a case against a couple of his fellow oligarchs back in Russia. Oligarchs that seemed to have less foresight and, maybe, less luck than Prokhorov always enjoyed. They, too, may well be forced to sell their assets but under very different circumstances.

Deripaska's life has been full of contradictions and struggles. Officially, he resides with his family and two kids. Living in a neighborhood where all the big shots of Russia live. He married into the powerful Yeltsin family. Yet he comes from very simple background, without any connections or wealth. He loves the countryside and the farms he grew up with and dislikes the office life he sometimes endures in Moscow. His piercing blue eyes depict a deep intellectual grasp—he is someone who mingles with the elites in Davos—but these are the same eyes that saw violence and murder the equal of any organized crime tactics.

With his tall stature (he measures six feet in height), deep voice, distinct forehead and full facial hair, he resembles more the proverbial Russian bear than an international businessman who competes with the giants of mining companies like BHP or Rio Tinto Group.

He has had all the status symbols of a Russian oligarch. Private jets, yachts, and mansions around the globe. He organizes elaborate events for his friends and business partners with endless champagne and beautiful Russian waitresses. Yet, he is not really attached to brands or eccentric demonstrations of wealth in a manner we might expect, considering his rank and wealth in Russia.

Over the years, his work has brought him to the exclusive rooms at the Kremlin in Moscow and to the smelters in the deepest snow deserts of the Siberian hinterlands. He has influential friends beyond Russia, foremost in Europe, the US and the UK. With Lord Gregory Barker, he had an influential proponent to get EN+ listed on the London Stock Exchange, one of his highest achievements. His reach went as far as to the highest echelons of Washington, and some say even to the current president, Donald Trump. The same connections that brought him power, influence and fame would seal his final downfall.

# PART TWO
# LESSONS LEARNED

## CHAPTER 6
# ON GENERAL SUCCESS AND FAILURE

In the following chapter, I would like to summarize some of the life lessons we can take away from the ten lives we discussed in Part I. Please keep in mind that the list is neither complete nor scientific proof that there are irrevocable and unquestionable consequences for specific actions we take when it comes to general success or managing your money. Even though many of our characters suffered horrendous financial blunders, their earning power always helped them overcome even the most challenging of situations. Johnny Depp and Winston Churchill are prime examples, and even Batista and Deripaska have more money after bankruptcy than a normal person like you or me. Nevertheless, their lives can give us clues, starting points and inspiration to make better decisions.

We should also remember that nothing is set in stone: fortunes can change, and people recover from their mistakes and misdeeds. Deripaska could find the old glories and respect that he so craved after. Even Eike Batista could make a miraculous comeback—we can be pretty confident that he has some cash stashed away. A glorious return of the old charmer is far from out of the question. MW hired the kind of professional help that will enable him to take charge of his own financial situation. Conversely, those surfing the waves of financial glory could lose their balance so easily, both through their own actions and through circumstances beyond their control.

### *Lesson #1 Education & Training*

#### *Education*

On all counts, Keynes is a posterchild of Western, high-end education. Attendance at the self-styled leading school in the world (in terms of status, if not education)—Eton and later Cambridge—he personifies the middle class and aristocratic elite of the British educational system. Success there laid the ground work for Keynes to win the Nobel Prize in economics, and on to his own personal fortune.

Even Churchill, to whom the education system was an anathema, took essential life skills away from his early schooling and then military training. From there, winning Nobel Prizes for both Literature and Peace shows that it is not necessary to be an A-grade student to achieve success—financial and otherwise—in life.

In fact, all of the characters we studied earlier who came from a business background had a good education. The same might not be true of all of our sporting and artistic characters. LeBron James had to pass his high school certificate, but only so that he could enter the world of professional basketball. But if the traditional system of education failed him, he continued to learn through his life experiences and his personal commitment to improving himself. The same could well be said for Johnny Depp.

These two might have been the opposite of, say, Keynes or MW when it came to formal schooling, but each has been a lifelong student of their own particular arts. For LeBron, whether his personal interest has been in business or investing, or charity and philanthropic causes—he has always been proactive in the search for knowledge.

The lesson we can take is that education is important in securing financial success, but that learning does not have to be through a traditional route of school and college.

#### *Training*

On-going training, as part of our lives, is vital to our potential success, just as it has been for LeBron James, Johnny Depp and Jennifer Lawrence. In fact, the commitment to the perfection of existing skills, and the development of new ones, are consistently-found traits among our group of well-known characters.

Regarding Depp and Lawrence, both might have been the leading talents of their generation, yet their natural ability still had to be shaped into something great. Only relentless training and guidance from mentors ensured that they become the Hollywood stars we today know.

Education and, as an extension of this, training in the field we choose is both elementary and a path that still leads to success even now, in the 21st century.

### *Lesson #2 Follow Your Passion*

Churchill was neither a talented student nor a very ambitious one. When at school, he possessed the charms of an opossum that many of his classmates tried to avoid at all cost. But what he sometimes lacked in tact, he compensated for with passion and military training.

He showed an early interest in all things military, and even though he wasn't an outstanding cadet in the traditional sense, he showed enormous valor and courage in the face of danger when facing the enemy. He retained these character traits throughout his career, always eager to visit the frontlines during both World Wars, and prior to this, battles in Africa. Indeed, he had to be persuaded not to be in the first wave of attacking allied soldiers who landed on the beaches of Normandy in 1944.

Today's more liberal voices would criticize such vigor for all things military. They shouldn't. These were different times, where traits like these for a young man his age were still highly regarded. They would, ultimately, turn Churchill into the wartime Prime Minister his country so much needed at the time most desperate in its history—facing Nazi Germany.

He also developed and retained a passion for literature. He laid the foundation of a very profitable career writing early on his life. Another passion of his was to impress his father, himself a highly successful political leader renowned for his bullying wit. While Churchill never felt he succeeded in doing this, it was a driving passion that stayed with him even after his father's early death.

Batista was convinced about his countries hidden treasures. He was passionate about what Brazil had to offer in terms of natural resources and opportunities. In an interview with The New York Times, he called Brazil his race horse. He believed that his country had the potential to become as rich as America. They may not be there yet, but Brazil is today one of the world's most influential emerging economies.

There is no denying that James, MW, Depp and Lawrence are passionate in their life callings. It's the energy they exude that seems to pull others towards them like a sun's attraction to other planets through gravitation. In its own way, the same passion can be seen in Carlos Slim and both of the Russian oligarchs we studied.

Passion gives us a sense of purpose, an elementary vision in life that can propel us forward. It might not offer the micro details about which business school is best, but it does offer a powerful macro vision. Once moving, there is a good chance that details will automatically fall in place.

With passion comes focus. Elementary discipline and commitment to doing things we most of the time prefer not to do. Passion empowers us to move forward and be active; it takes away passivity and stagnation. When we have passion, the tasks about which we will normally procrastinate become readily tackled.

### *Lesson #3 The Importance of Courage*

Churchill was a complex character, but he was filled with traditional values such as valor, bravery and courage.

Keynes showed enormous courage by publishing his book on the treaty. He clearly understood the career risks involved and the enemies his book would make. Yet he wrote it nevertheless, because he had the courage to do the right thing. He could see the whole farce that was economic thinking at that time. His financial success, world recognition and lasting respect would prove him right.

Batista referred to himself as the "truffle sniffing Labrador"; if that was true, he was a Labrador with a fine nose. But what marked him in his early years was boldness and courage to follow his instincts. A personal vision. He was always a risk taker who experienced luck in almost everything he did. He literally struck gold in the depth of the Amazon jungle. But he needed courage for that. However, there is a fine line between courage and controlled risk-taking compared to the excessively irresponsible risks that lead to hubris, as we shall see later

### *Lesson #4 Never Give Up*

Keynes learned from his financial mistakes, like a scientist adjusting his formula, tweaking here and changing this and that. In the end, it led to an understanding of the complex factor of mass psychology in his perfect mathematical calculation and theory framework. This, too, he would account for and with great success.

LeBron James overcame the adversity of a tough upbringing, with a single mom and no permanent home.

Batista had drive, ambition and vision… and a determination to succeed. He was hardworking and had an ability to project laser-like focus on key projects—all important attributes of a successful entrepreneur, leader and visionary. He learned to deal with setbacks and he had the drive to overcome them. He needed all those characteristics in a business that didn't take prisoners and lived in a culture that dated back to the days of the California Gold Rush.

Deripaska's approach to crisis management is admirable. His drive and determination to face challenges offers a lesson that will continue to be followed. His war room and his dealings with Putin himself are worthy of a Hollywood movie. He will need it all again, as he faces his largest challenge yet.

Churchill sums up the lesson of never giving up best: It takes courage to hold a position, and not to weaken our grip upon it. This was perhaps Churchill's most distinguished character trait: to never give up.

### *Lesson #5 Invest in Relationships*

Prokhorov and Deripaska each certainly knew how to play the power game. Deripaska realized early on that powerful relationships are key to success on a grand level. Like other members of Russia's new business elite, Deripaska built strong ties to the state and political leaders. His early business entanglements with the Cherney brothers (and Michael, in particular) gave him several strategic advantages, political protection, financial resources and access to new contacts.

His marriage to Polina Yumasheva, a relative to former president Boris Yeltsin, might have been based on love, but it didn't hurt his career aspirations either. And even though his close ties to the Kremlin might haunt him now, his loyalty to the relationships he nurtured will guarantee their support in his home country.

Eike Batista has always had a natural charisma. He possesses an innate gift to schmooze and endear himself to others, and he projects the self-image to back this up. He proved his natural talents over and over again in his eventful career, charming bankers, investors and business partners and even elderly German ladies—not to mention the Brazilian people... and a long row of supermodels. Over the years, he perfected his salesmanship, as he used his elaborate, pretentious lifestyle cleverly to manipulate public opinion about himself and his business endeavors. According to some sources, he learned these skills early on as an insurance salesman in Germany while still being an engineering student, where his ability to soft talk elderly ladies was legendary.[102]

### *Family and Friends*

Classic self-help books describe it as surrounding yourself with the right people. They don't usually pull their punches.

Choose your friends wisely and dump those that are deadweight! Surround yourself with people who cheer you up, motivate and push you forward. Lose people who drag you down.

I would elaborate on these statements with a more diplomatic overtone. Invest in and maintain key relationships. Success in life might originate from within all of us, but to give it wings we need others, including friends and family.

Carlos Slim always enjoyed his family life. His upbringing, his own family, and now the families of his children have all been a great source of joy. And thus, support.

For Jennifer Lawrence, her immediate family is a constant source of inspiration, a gauge on how her life is really going, based on her personal barometer—values that seem to be old-fashioned among the Hollywood elite.

My best advice is to surround yourself with people with common sense and whom you can trust. Nurturing the right relationships has worked throughout the ages, and will continue to serve successful people well.

### *Lesson #6 Success Doesn't Discriminate*

LeBron James overcame enormous odds. He had God-given talents—his physical size and his magnificent sporting skills—but he had to overcome social and racial discrimination to achieve his place atop the mountain. Discrimination should never be allowed as an excuse; rather, it's a hurdle we have to overcome, making us a stronger person in the process.

Lawrence has fought gender discrimination in Hollywood all her life. And even though she scored some success, Hollywood is far from being truly gender equal. Her fight will continue, as it will for many women across the employment sector. Lawrence succeeded as one of the world's highest-earning actresses because she didn't let discrimination get in her way to the top.

Both Prokhorov and Deripaska overcame enormous social barriers within their native Russia. Although it claimed to be a socialist country, where everyone is equal by definition, it was riddled with discrimination among the political elite and established classes throughout communist history. Both Prokhorov and Deripaska succeeded because they didn't let their backgrounds get in their way; instead, it motivated them to succeed through their work, wits and connections.

Even, Keynes and Churchill had to overcome discrimination. Keynes was middle class, but his family was financially stretched and looked down upon by the aristocratic elite of the time. Churchill might have been a person with aristocratic privileges, but he too had to overcome social discrimination within his own class and from his peers. His father's political legacy weighed heavily on Winston, and one of his life goals was to clean up his family's reputation.

We live in a world littered with discrimination. It is easy to use this as an excuse for failing to reach our goals. Discrimination is insidious and unfair, but it can be turned into motivation for our own success.

### Lesson #7 Money Follows, But It May Not Stay with You!

As the Joker said in The Dark Knight, "If you are good at something, never do it for free." All our examples were good at something and they all got paid.

For Churchill, although there was money—and history—in his family, he made his fortune largely off his own work.

So did Keynes, who was recognized early on by people in

academia and government. Keynes and Churchill both achieved early financial success because they were recognized for their skills and passion for their subject matter. They were not afraid to promote themselves in order to get recognition. In fact, this generalization can be applied for every one of our ten case studies.

While we might not become a LeBron James, a Nobel Prize winner or an oligarch, by following the rules so far outlined, we will get recognition.

The next stage is to combine this with the elementary courage to ask for compensation for what we do. Many of us dislike self-promotion, feeling uncomfortable at blowing our own horn. But it is necessary to gain the rewards we deserve.

### *Failure Factors*

While failure is as much a part of life as success, and all ten characters experienced their fair share of setbacks, five cases illustrate the effects of failure in a serious way.

Firstly, why do so many other sports celebrities fail with their finances?

The simple reasoning behind it is that many sports celebrities make it big early in their lives. It seems as though they have it all, but lack the worldliness to keep it safe.

It is a truism that many sports stars are from humble backgrounds; achieving financial security when still relatively young means that the wish to compensate for their early struggles is overwhelming The list of sports celebrities who spent their fortunes on too many luxuries—fast cars, multiple houses, expensive jewelry, even yachts—is extensive. It includes, among many others, Jack Clark of baseball fame, NBA star Allen Iverson, boxer Mike Tyson and tennis legend Boris Becker.

The most common explanation offered for this is a lack of financial literacy, sometimes connected to their educational level. Most athletes make it big after finishing high school. From this foundation, they have little or even no sound financial background to help them manage their huge revenue windfalls. Therefore, they assign too much work to their financial managers and risk abuse or misuse of their assets.

While the above certainly offer some explanations, overspending alone doesn't tell the whole picture, nor does it provide a conclusive reason for personal bankruptcy. Neither is this phenomenon reserved to sports celebrities or personalities with poor upbringings. There is much more behind this than meets the eye.

Movie stars, medical doctors and even world politicians can be as much a victim as a sports star. It seems it has more to do with a general lack of interest than with their educational background or intellectual grasp. Churchill, arguably one of the smartest politicians of his time, had as much financial grasp of his personal finances as MW had of his. They were both terrible with their personal finances. Worse, their better halves didn't provide any checks and balances that work in many marriages. Spouses often provide a counterweight to their partner's lack of interest in the subject matter or their tendency to overspend and gamble. MW's wife justified their financial illiteracy on the basis of their intellectual standing in society, suggesting that doctors never care about money. Churchill's wife, in many regards a perfect wife, had as much influence on his gambling trips as his political enemies had on his daring political and military campaigns. He just ignored them both, even though a hearty kick in his private parts by his wife would have certainly worked wonders.

Financial failure is often a result of:
1. Chronic overspending that leads to debt
2. The tendency to gamble
3. No control and oversight with checks and balances

In short, they are simply bad with money, often not being fully in control of their own finances. We can extract some valuable lessons from those who committed enormous personal and financial blunders.

### *Lesson #8 Greed, the Icarus Factor—Flying Too Close to the Sun*

Greed is a powerful weapon for bad. Common sense, rational decision-making and day-to-day business operations all suffer as a result of uncontrollable greed. Batista and Deripaska, some might argue, are two people from whom we can learn a little about this vice.

In Batista's case, even though the details of his life story are complicated, the saga of his success and downfall is surprisingly simple. Batista made most of his fortune during the commodities booms. His phenomenal success was built both on mountains of debt and his ability to schmooze bankers and investors. Batista was always in a hurry to capture the opportunity and maximize profits. But this meant that his empire was built on shifting sands, and it took little movement for his foundations to collapse. He seems to have failed to learn the lesson of his first major financial setback, which was with TBX.

Deripaska, too, sought to enlarge his empire beyond sustainable levels. His own expansion—acquiring numerous businesses—placed this darling of the Russian investment banks in a tricky predicament. The purchase of Norilsk Nickel and the changing market conditions of 2008 were the last nails in his coffin.

On Wall Street, financial losses are often explained through the greed of their market participants. It can capture the CEO of the Fortune 500 company as easily as it captures the investment banker, the doctor or even the shoeshine boy. Greed and megalomania are a common cause for financial blunders and in this book, we have plenty of examples. Even Keynes showed signs of greed as he misjudged the devastating effects of financial leverage when positions went against him.

## Lesson #9 Gullibility, or Lack of Common Sense

Greed is universal. It can manifest itself in different ways, and its victims often display one of two traits: gullibility or extreme over-confidence, neither of which is something to be proud of.

Johnny Depp is a good example of a person used to the good life, but one who did not wish to get involved in its intricacies. Instead, he trusted the dirty details to his outside management companies, who repaid his trust and lack of oversight by cheating him on fees and with bad financial advice. A man who seems to have little interest in his finances, and no financial roadmap, might well be described as gullible.

While it is wrong to generalize, elite athletes can be another example of this phenomenon. Usually, young adults leave the important financial decisions to their managers, tax or investment advisors for a good reason. Though many of these service companies give sound advice, their wealthy clients' lack of financial acumen and interest in such matters can mean that they find it hard to distinguish between credible and misleading advice.

In many cases, they give complete power of attorney in practically all important financial matters. Again, there is nothing fundamentally wrong with this, but oversight of their finances and their own personal financial development does not take place. Common sense comes through experience, and that is not developed when all financial decisions are outsourced.

It is not just young athletes or Hollywood stars who can be gullible. MW and his wife, including many of their friends in the wealthy circles of Munich, have become victims of fraud in one form or another. The simple Ponzi scheme to which the MWs fell victim is just a minor financial part of the bigger blunder they committed. Being defrauded by a lifelong family friend ranks on a totally different level, psychologically and financially.

Even the rich and famous follow their whims, and they jump blindly onto the bandwagon. Some are easily convinced to go into trendy investment schemes by very skilled salespeople, who play their client's gullible tendencies to perfection. None has been more notorious in modern times than Bernard Madoff. [103] He is the mastermind behind the largest Ponzi scheme in history. I highly recommend reading some of the books that give a full account what happened within Madoff's operation, the psychological profiles of his many victims, and what happened to his clients' money in the end.

### *Lesson #10 Hubris*

When dealing with greed, we have extreme self-confidence at the other end of the spectrum. Self-confidence can easily turn into hubris, and that in turn can lead to financial disaster.

There is probably nothing more devastating in human history than the effects of hubris. The old Greeks were well aware of it, as were philosophers and writers of their time (including Plutarch), who warned about it.

Hubris is defined as excessive self-confidence or pride, and leads to making overly risky bets or to ignoring relevant warning signs and failure to invoke contingency plans.[104] It is "outrageous arrogance" in the light of success and rising overconfidence. In the real world, success in one area leads to overconfidence in others—for example, money.

Churchill is a good example. As a military leader, his

brinkmanship was perhaps the only way to defeat a more powerful and infinitely wicked enemy. But it served him badly in his financial life.

But it wasn't only Churchill who fell into the trap of hubris. Keynes was equipped with ample self-confidence. Rightly so, as his intellectual and rigorous academic approach was unmatched. Among his peers (and later in government), he was soon recognized for his supreme overconfidence. At times he got too cocky, as his early trading operations nearly wiped him out twice, so that he even had to put his beloved art collection up for auction. His overconfidence in his own skills and intellectual superiority made him believe he could play the markets like Isaac Newton played the stars. He was wrong and paid for it dearly. But unlike other protagonists, he recognized his mistakes and learned from those flaws.

Batista twice underestimated how sensitive his entire operation was to shifting commodity cycles and outside macroeconomics factors. He underestimated the enormous financial, as well as political, risks in a country that is far from stable. But ultimately, these flaws would reveal his greatest weaknesses: his lack of sound financial principles and his inability to stop and consolidate his wealth and influence underlying his business empire and wealth.

Deripaska's supreme confidence in his skills and contacts in Moscow led him to underestimate the complex financial nature of his transactions, increasing his already debt-laden empire with more debt. He underestimated the resilience and tenacity of Potanin as a serious opponent, both financially and politically.

### *Lesson #11 Lies, Lies, Lies*

Lies are as much a part of human society as the forbidden fruit was to Adam and Eve. Lies might give us a short-term advantage, but haunt us in the long-term. They usually strike back with a vengeance. Certainly, the most common form of lie, which seeks to gain an unfair advantage over others, can often be traced back to financial blunders and personal failure.

Eike Batista, who was driven by his ambition to be the richest man on the planet, started to mislead investors early on. He knew that his oil deposits could not produce the amount of oil he claimed. His empire was already crumbling, something to which he could not admit.

Worst of all is lying to ourselves. Such denial of reality can lead to huge personal failure. These lies are much more complex and more difficult to detect and to counteract. As Psychology Today writes:

> "Self-deception, or lying to yourself, is simply a motivated false belief. False beliefs can satisfy important psychological needs of the individual (e.g., confidence in one's abilities)."[105]

Ignorance, reality denial and overconfidence are all symptoms, in one way or another, of lying to yourself.

Deep down, I am sure, Churchill knew he was bad in handling his own money. But facing up to it, to seek help or council from those who could have brought order to his personal finances and saved him many public embarrassments, seemed out of the question in Churchill's lifetime.

MW knew deep down that his life and passion lay with treating his patients and seeking intellectual and cultural stimulation. It was not to be found mingling with bankers and business people. However, he wasn't strong enough to face reality and cut his losses.

If self-deception is taken too far, it can lead to more than just financial blunders—it can destroy lives.

## Chapter 7
# FIVE MONEY LESSONS

From Part I, there are two pieces of core understanding we need to take into this chapter:

1. Financial success from your profession doesn't guarantee continuous financial success beyond. Making, keeping and managing your wealth are distinctively separate skills that need to be honed.
2. Money skills represent an abstract skill set that even the most educated and intelligent have difficulty in mastering.

If we look at all the case studies in this book, we see that each had to generate and manage their income and later their considerable wealth. For each of these phases, they needed different approaches and skill sets. Therefore, I would like to divide them into three phases for the process of becoming and staying wealthy:

1. The earnings phase
2. The managing your earnings phase
3. The managing your wealth phase

Around these three phases, I have summarized the following five lessons about money, which include the core skills necessary to master each phase. They are drawn from the lessons of success and financial blunders of our protagonists. These five core lessons come with some suggestions and possible solutions to how you could incorporate them into your own life to reach your financial goals. These goals can ultimately deliver financial freedom.

### *Lesson #1 Investing in Yourself: Be Your Own Cash Engine*

Each of our case studies shows that the protagonists had some form of high level education or training that enabled each of them to earn a high income in one form or another. No other than Churchill demonstrates the importance of being your most important source of income. For him, it was writing that always lifted him out of financial difficulties, something he couldn't have done without an early investment in his formal education and later following his passion for reading and writing.

Depp is lucky that his brand is still intact, even though it's tarnished. He is an outstanding actor and he will get future roles; he only needs to adjust his spending habits and take care of his money by simplifying the process of his money's management, avoiding fancy financial schemes.

Certainly, besides his theoretical knowledge about metallurgy and mining, Eike Batista had enormous talents in salesmanship that he perfected over the years, starting with charming old ladies into buying insurance in Germany to charming politicians, bankers and investors. If he hadn't gambled big, lied and thus destroyed his reputation, he might still be charming world dignitaries and the wealthy of Brazil today.

### *Actions*

First, you need to invest in your own earnings potential. That means focus on your education and training first to hone your primary earning potential. Through continuous strategic investments in yourself, such as higher education, an old-fashioned apprenticeship or specialized training, you can increase your own earning power. You can volunteer for experience by offering your work for free. In the end, you will be able to generate stable income.

Many feel that the biggest challenge is to find the right calling, the hidden passion in life that'll would makes us excel at the highest level. This lack of passion—of finding what is right for them—can often be used as an excuse for failing at their education. Though true to some extent, this argument should never be used as an excuse for passivity and indecisiveness. In fact, it's not the challenge of finding the right calling, but rather having the commitment to see their work through to the end.

The notion of a one-and-only calling is a misconception in my view, as throughout life our circumstances change, and we change too. However, our education and initial training provide us with the core skills and tools to survive and flourish in any future endeavors we might choose for ourselves. So, my advice is to see your education to the end, get the training that is offered to you, even though it might not be the initial passion you have hoped for. You will still have plenty of time in your life to find the right calling that offers fulfillment...and money!

For the same reasons, and using the same philosophy, I advise that you continue investing in yourself, using on-going education and training. Follow the advice of Australian television presenter, Paul Clitheroe: "Invest in yourself. Your career is the engine of your wealth."

### *Lesson #2 Budgeting*

When Churchill was finally laid to rest on January 24, 1965, at the grand age of 90, the world mourned. England mourned him for a week. It is generally believed that some mourned because they had lost a huge customer in Winston Churchill.[106] Nicholas Cage once blew $150 million on a private island and a dinosaur skull. Johnny Depp blasted the remains of his good friend into space. Mike Tyson has made headlines for buying exotic pets, million-dollar bathtubs, and a fleet of luxurious cars—about 110 of them in all.

At the other end of the spectrum, we have Jay Leno, former host of The Tonight Show, who seems to be managing his money with some strict rules. Apparently, although having hosted the show since way back in 1992, he still lived on a smaller, secondary income from other part-time jobs. He never touched the money from his job as the host. "When I got The Tonight Show, I always made sure I did 150 [comedy show] gigs a year so I never had to touch the principal," Leno says. To this day, he's never touched any of the money earned from The Tonight Show. You can imagine that he must have saved a lot of money earned from one of America's most popular late-night talk shows. At his career height, he reportedly received about $30 million a year. [107]

Although Leno's efforts are noteworthy and admirable, it's not the way most of us can or should live our lives. Certainly, spending is all relative. What might look like excessive spending for an average person might be a drop in a wide ocean of water for a persona like Bill Gates, LeBron James or a Russian oligarch. The key is to balance our spending with the income we know we have, allowing us to allocate money based on future earnings potential. Anybody can earn money, and if you end up spending less than you make, you have a positive cash flow, which can be either spent, saved or ideally reinvested.

### *Actions*

There are a couple of tasks you need to do to make the right financial decisions for yourself. Assessing your earning power and taking an inventory of all your personal assets is vital. Unless we are sure about our income situation and our financial reserves, we won't be able to avoid unnecessary risk.

**Keep records:** Carlos Slim was taught the importance of financial discipline and record keeping by his father. He still has the first accounting ledger he maintained as a young boy that showed income and spending.

Record keeping requires a certain amount of diligence and discipline, but it is nothing that an average person cannot do. Modern software, from PC software to apps for smartphone devices, offers endless choices. They can assist by taking most of the pain of recording or summarizing the financial damage you caused each week! Others, like me personally, prefer excel spreadsheets that often mutate into colorful beasts of tables, formulas and charts.

The most important aspect of budgeting is not the skill of performing it, but the attitude of doing it on a regular basis. Follow the Nike slogan: "Just do it"—at least once a month!

**Curb your spending:** This especially important in the beginning phase, where every dollar we have might actually yield a very high return in the future. Better, use any dollar not spent on any reasonable investment project: education, training, your own business or traditional forms of investment. Once you have your records straight, you can easily identify areas where you could cut spending or even allocate more money to any of your investment projects. Overspending, as those celebrities and mega-wealthy did, will never be an issue when you have income-producing assets to support that spending. But without any assets in the first place, it will be difficult to ever reach a sustainable expenditure level.

**Avoid debt:** It is especially important to avoid consumer debt. Connected to curbing spending is avoiding debt to finance that spending. Yes, we can take out a mortgage on our house, we can make use of credit cards, and yes, we can take out loans to pay for our student fees. The point here is to check the numbers, to be aware of the financial responsibilities we have and to simplify our financial management. Avoiding debt simplifies everything. It's important to keep in mind to balance the amount of debt we manage with the income and assets we have. To live within our means still has relevance, even today, despite debt levels reaching new highs.

Get your financial house in order first by measuring and assessing it. Periodically go over these numbers. It will train you to take charge of your financial affairs, which is, ultimately, the single most important step in creating an investment plan. Check your current and potential earning power and keep track of expenses. Equally important is the matter of saving to accumulate assets and to build a strong financial base for future investing. Saving works. If there is not enough money for future financial needs such as retirement, you either save more money, work more, work longer, or you create additional earnings opportunities over time, so that you can save more in the future. Simple home budgeting will go a long way.

## *Lesson #3 Learning the Principles of Investment*

Among the most skilled investors included in this book were Carlos Slim, Maynard Keynes and Mikhail Prokhorov. On the surface, they made enormous financial decisions and took enormous risks, but always came out ahead by having higher cash flows and higher asset valuation prices.

On the other hand, we saw investment failures such as MW, Johnny Depp and Winston Churchill, where their investment decisions caused horrific financial blunders.

Carlos Slim represents the best example of having the ideal investment strategy. Starting from being in control of his finances, he accumulated savings that he would invest in cash flow-strong opportunities, i.e., assets that produce income and can appreciate in price, among them real estate in his home town of Mexico. No better example of his learnings and personal application can be found than in the crisis of 1982.

Slim, in effect, made a huge bet on the future of his home country (that was basically wiped off the economic surface of the world), believing that Mexico would survive the most severe recession to date. Who could have made this kind of investment except a native of Mexico, a person who understood the ins and outs of his economy, the business community, and its leaders? A decade later, he would invest most of his money in Telmex when it was up for auction—a once-in-a-lifetime opportunity that Slim took. His strategy evolved from understanding cash flows, unique opportunities, and getting good prices.

On the other hand, we have negative examples, such as Batista and Deripaska, but also Churchill, MW and Johnny Depp. Churchill's tendency to make brash decisions with his money—his unnecessary risk-taking in his financial affairs—would present an unsolvable conundrum for his wife and himself. MW and Johnny Depp wouldn't make any decisions for themselves at all, just passing the responsibility on to people whom they believed could take care of their money—each suffering some devastating results.

Churchill, Keynes and Deripaska are good examples of a "forced seller". This is someone short on cash, or being forced to liquidate assets in a hurry without having the luxury to wait for fair pricing. The two main reasons for forced sellers are declining market prices and over-leverage. Even if the owner of the asset knew its real economic value, in these situations there is no choice other than to sell it back to the market in order to get the liquidity he is forced to generate. Keynes had to liquidity his entire positions, twice, because he got margin calls. Deripaska was called in by bank, twice as well, to reduce his debt and sell his assets in acts of emergency. So did Batista, when he faced massive liquidity constraints due to falling commodity prices and bank recalls. This phenomenon applies as much to professional investment managers including hedge funds as it does to all social classes, from the average consumer constantly in debt, to the billionaire who has overleveraged himself and will go bankrupt in a matter of months.

From Keynes, we can learn that speculation is a dangerous game—particularly with borrowed money. Keynes thought he could play the fluctuations in currency and commodity markets with his "superior knowledge." It may be easy enough to digest a ream of statistics and figures about past and present market conditions, but your research may have no predictive value for the future.

Instead, he became an investor in businesses, with little or no leverage, with a long-term view on corporate earnings rather than on trying to forecast the next market price move. Keynes had started honing his new investment policy long before the war, having found ways to endure and bounce back from the market routs after 1929. He would establish an investment policy similar to Slim's by understanding the underlying assets, the opportunity to acquire them, and at a price that made economic sense. Time would do the rest—as we know, he died a very wealthy economist.

### *Actions*

You don't have to be a Warren Buffett, a George Soros, the famous hedge fund manager, or computer math wizard programming high-powered AI. You just need to learn the principles of investing and most importantly, to distinguish between gambling (speculation) and investment. There is no better example than LeBron James, who made a conscious effort to learn this... and to learn it from the best by calling out Warren Buffett, publicly.

**Distinguish between gambling and investing:** Investing means to lay out money today to receive income in the future, and ideally, regular income during the time you lay out your money. In the simplest terms, we spend our money on assets that can produce regular income. Gambling or professional speculation means to hope for an event happening in the future over which you have no control. In its most basic form it means to speculate on price changes in financial markets. Often such speculation is based on incomplete and faulty assumptions and research.

Investing, by definition, is about making bets on an uncertain future, but with a conscious effort to manage those risks by understanding the probability of cash flows. In an ideal world, these cash inflows accumulate each month and build the basis of our personal wealth. From this comes future investment. But there is more to it. With each future investment you make, you should be able to increase your free cash flow through investment income and capital gains, reinforcing the positive cycle of income growth and wealth accumulation. It all starts with your primary cash engine.

**Understand the probabilities of cash inflows:** The probability of success in investment comes from understanding cash flows and the price we have to pay for them today. The skill set here lies in understanding and finding these characteristics in assets we want to acquire—these are called investment opportunities. This can be a tricky activity that requires specialized education and training as an investor. However, today there are investment products that greatly help to simplify this procedure and that promise satisfactory returns with limited financial risk. All you need to do is to make a purchasing decision and not to panic in times of adverse market movements. More on this in the next lesson.

Never become a forced seller: There is nothing worse in investing than being forced to sell at the worst possible moment - usually at times of market declines - and being right in the long-term. Prokhorov might have been a forced seller, but he was extremely lucky and I am sure he knows this. You never want to be forced to sell and you never want to experience unforced errors, which, like in tennis, are "entirely a result of the player's own blunder and not because of the opponent's skill or effort."[108] To avoid ever getting yourself in such a precarious situation follow Buffett's simple advice to LeBron James: "Somebody in his position ought to have a significant cash reserve."[109] You always want to operate from a basis of financial strength, and the easiest way to achieve this is to have plenty of cash reserves (liquidity) and cash inflows from existing investments. So ignore the conventional advice of being invested with all your money at all times or even use financial leverage to maximize your potential gains. Instead, always keep cash reserves and buy when others are forced to sell.

*Lesson #4 Simplify Money Management*

Johnny Depp was never really interested in managing his money by himself. No wonder—his reckless spending and poor choices of investments made it a mammoth task for any accountant or financial advisor (though a lucrative one). On top of this, his accountants had to manage the usual levels of complication when it comes to making savings through complex tax shelters. These tax shelters might be perfectly legal, but present insurmountable challenges to a person who has little interest in his/her financial situation.

MW and his wife couldn't believe that their old friend and the family's legal counsel cheated them for years on fees, depriving them of the financial benefits they had hoped for. After detailed investigations, the MWs found a web of complicated legal structures about which they weren't even aware.

Churchill did not successfully curb his reckless spending, even though he tried with certain measures that did not last for long. We cannot blame him for this or even criticize his rather elaborate spending habits and taste for the good and cultured life, with cigars and brandies and meat and even art. After all, he was an aristocrat, a politician, and a gentleman.

But what we could blame him for was his lack of understanding of making prudent financial decisions. Had he kept all his money from all the royalties and endowments he received and invested them very conservatively in fixed income securities or in things he understood, he could have easily financed his elaborate lifestyle. By just simplifying his money management and not gambling on things he neither understood (stock market) nor had control over (such as his trips to Monaco), he wouldn't have needed elaborate advice, financial help from friends, or lengthy discussions with the tax man.

Keynes, on the other hand, finally understood that financial leverage on unsure bets could be devastating. He radically changed his investment approach by simplifying everything to the point that he conducted his investment affairs out of his bed each day for an hour.[110] He simply invested in enterprises he understood, were profitable and could be purchased at a discount to what there were really worth. In so doing, he improved the odds of winning... and winning he did.

This might still have been beyond LeBron James abilities early in his career as a successful entrepreneur and investor, but he knew whom to ask for advice. He reached out to the most successful investor alive—Warren Buffett—and The Oracle of Omaha had some financial advice for the NBA superstar:

> *"Through the rest of his career and beyond, in terms of earning power, [he should] just make monthly investments in the low-cost index fund," Buffett told CNBC's Squawk Box ... in response to a video question posed by James. "Somebody in his position ought to have a significant cash reserve."*[111]

Buffett's reasoning is simple and makes a lot of sense. Index funds are geared towards profiting from US businesses and the US economy. Historically over long periods of time, they have yielded between 7% and 9% per year. They are transparent and low cost, making them ideal for individual investors with a more passive inclination. You can either buy them through one of the leading fund providers directly, such as Vanguard or BlackRock or buy them via an ETF structure from the stock exchange through your brokerage account. They might not be sexy for everyone, but they do what they promise: to cover your investment basics and simplify your investment management.

### *Actions*

Simplify your money management buy sticking to the basics. Earn your money, save it and occasionally deploy it in investment opportunities you understand and feel comfortable with. Savings accounts and fixed-term papers are simple, and they work even in low-interest rate environments. It's never a bad idea to keep some of that money in physical gold. If you feel you can stomach the ups and downs of stock market fluctuations, buy simple index funds. If you periodically invest in US index funds, you might not become a Jeff Bezos or Warren Buffett, but you won't end up like Mike Tyson or Nicholas Cage either. Follow Buffett's advice "...usually, the simplest is the best."

### *Lesson #5 Knowing Yourself*

One of my clients, who is a professional racing pilot, once showed me his impressive collection of rare sports cars. For every car he bought, he had a background story, he remembered the price he paid, and what they were worth today. It became clear that his fleet of rare and valuable cars had increased substantially in value. There is no doubt that he understands the opportunities in this niche market and he knows how to negotiate each purchase and sale. He is an expert in this field and he has therefore been increasing his wealth.

Keynes was an avid collector of fine art and rare antiques. He had an eye for value and in the process, accumulated impressive collections. Had he just saved up his income and bought rare collectables only, he would have become wealthy in his own right.

Both examples illustrate probably the most important lesson about money, one which isn't even directly connected to it. Know yourself. Know your strength and know your weaknesses, and here is why:

**Opportunity and the circle of competence:** Carlos Slim understood businesses, corporate finance and investing. In the process, he became the wealthiest man in Mexico and one of the richest in the world.

LeBron James' strength lies in practicing humility, learning from the best and rigorously applying it by practicing and drilling over and over again.

Batista, early on, specialized in metallurgy, mining and natural resources, all valuable skills in his native country of Brazil. It gave him an edge in negotiations and an eye for opportunity.

Prokhorov knew something about businesses and basketball. He combined both strengths in a very profitable business venture. The team might be lacking the sports success he hoped, but no one can deny Prokhorov's skill set in making deals and increasing the value of the franchise.

The world of money is a very competitive field and prone to manipulation and outright fraud. If you venture out into this realm, you need to start at the bottom, learn and gain experience. You can do that better if you make use of your natural given talents and interests. Make use of all their advantages and operate from a position of financial strength. Your strength comes from your primary skill set; develop it and let it grow so you can gain what Buffett calls a "circle of competence." Operate within that circle, and you will be able to operate from a position of strength. Financially as well as mentally. You will get better in identifying opportunities with a higher likelihood of winning. Ultimately, this will lead to wiser and smarter money decisions. Focus and develop your strengths and work on your weaknesses or avoid them altogether with the help of experts.

**Advisors:** Sometimes you have to face reality and be honest with yourself. You don't want to manage your money and you don't want to make financial decisions that will cause you sleepless nights—fine! That's not a problem if you follow some basic rules.

1. Take responsibility: Follow the basic money rules from above—there is simply no way around these money principles. You just can't avoid taking the bare minimum of financial responsibility.
2. Simplify: Aim to simplify the entire administration of your financial affairs by following the basics. Earn your salary, accumulate cash, buy fixed-term papers to get some interest and stash away some gold (between 5% to 10% of your net asset value). That's it! If you can stomach some market risk, follow Buffett's advice and buy some US or global stock index funds on a regular basis, e.g., quarterly.

With your simplified money management approach, there is also less room to complicate things from an accounting, tax or legal perspective. If you still need outside help due to specific financial and family circumstances, use outside professional advice and not the help from family and friends. If you can afford it, go for the best and most reputable tax and law firms. They might be expensive, but you can be assured that any blatant form of fraud is out of the question. Each has the investment expertise to provide you with solid investment advice based on risk diversification as well as tax and legal considerations. It's good to have two independent firms look over your finances from a different perspective, legal as well as tax—a second opinion never hurts. Both parties then provide additional oversight and control, which work as your personal checks and balances.

# Conclusions

In this book, we have seen the patterns of success and the patterns of financial blunders. Some of the lessons are as old as human history itself, and in the end, each new generation is condemned to make the same mistakes over and over again.

Luck and good fortune are as much part of life as misfortune, and it could strike at any moment! This is the fascinating part of life: everything is in flux and can change. Yet success and failure are as much a product of traditional values and principles as they were almost 2,000 years back, when Plutarch wrote his famous biographies of noble Romans and Greeks. This won't change any time soon.

We looked at ten very different lives from a wide range of backgrounds, skill sets, ages and even gender. All ten people can teach us something about success and failure. It comes in all shapes and sizes. In their own rights, they were all financially successful, either in their respective professions or business endeavors. They had financial success through a combination of unique skills and talents. Their hard work, courage and dedication helped them to convert raw talent and skill into financial success.

But all of them demonstrate quite clearly that they, too, are only human. People from all walks of life make money mistakes, even though some might have powerful advantages over the small guy. The rich and famous just commit mistakes on a different scale, but they are still human. Wealthy people make the same mistakes as we normal folks do.

We learned that getting wealthy is not the same as staying wealthy. Just because someone is successful in their own profession doesn't mean they become automatically a success in handling their own money affairs.

On the contrary, those who stayed wealthy followed some simple principles of money management and investing. More importantly, they had character traits that were conducive to continued financial success with the money they had already accumulated.

In each case, we saw that those who remained successful and avoided financial blunders understood themselves and acted accordingly with their money. They constructed money management and investment policies that incorporated their strength and lifestyles and income situation. What we observed was that the winners stayed involved and continued their self-education.

The ones who lost out were mainly passive in the self-education of handling their money, and left it to others or acted on impulse and whim. We also saw that the trust they placed in their advisors was oftentimes abused.

On the other end of the spectrum, we found the aggressive risk takers. Filled with overconfidence, they failed miserably. Overleveraging themselves, outright gambling or underestimating of effects of adverse economic developments were common features amongst this group.

### *What does that mean for you?*

The good news is that financial success comes down to only a very few decisions. The way to be successful with money is to stay actively involved in your financial management and investment activities—to take responsibility.

The bad news: How you approach this responsibility depends on personality and attitude towards the subject matter. If you suffer from self-delusion or have a general distaste for all things related to money, you might get yourself into serious financial trouble. Failure to address these shortcomings early on only magnifies the challenges ahead when your income rises.

Most of the time, we can become successful by just avoiding the main causes of failure. Here are some suggestions to avoid the four enemies of financial success…and success in general:

### *Against Gullibility*

A healthy dose of skepticism and independent thinking. Don't take everything for face value, especially about the latest money-making schemes, trendy investments or what your financial advisor tells you to buy. Take responsibility by following the basic principles of money and money management. It requires self-awareness.

### *Against Greed*

The only way against greed is to step back and assess your situation from different perspectives. A strategic retreat (time out) will enable you to contemplate your situation from a more neutral position.

### *Against Hubris*

The best antidote to hubris is humility. In his book, Only the Paranoid Survive, former Intel CEO Andy Grove said, "Success leads to its own demise." In other words, success is its own worst enemy. Humility reminds you that you are human, that you aren't perfect, and that you are bound to make mistakes or experience times of bad luck. Again, a strategic retreat can help to practice humility. It requires a lot of self-awareness.

### *Against Lies*

The answer is obvious but needs to be repeated over and over again. Don't lie! As the saying goes, the best policy is honesty, so you don't have to remember all your lies. Don't lie to others, but more importantly, don't lie to yourself. This, too, requires self-awareness.

### *Practice Self-Awareness*

As you have noticed, all solutions have one thing in common: self-awareness. The definition of self-awareness is "conscious knowledge of one's own character and feelings."

It means to know yourself and, at times, to be brutally honest with both yourself and others. Practice independent thinking and self-awareness that leads to independent decision-making and better decision-making. Remember, nothing defines us more than the decisions we make. Especially for money!

# Afterword

I hope this book unraveled some of the complexity of a topic as abstract as success and money, and I hope it will help you on your quest to make better decisions when it comes to your financial life. Each lesson we learn from the case studies in this book just scratches the surface in their respective field. Each biography alone could and has covered entire libraries. The subjects of personal finance and investment are widely covered in the multitude of self-help books that proliferate today. There are plenty of learning and training videos available on and offline.

Today, there is a wide variety of content out there, often free of charge, from written documents and books to audio recordings to video online courses. I highly encourage you to continue your studies—especially in the field of personal money management—if you are truly interested in financial success.

When choosing the 10 lives for this book, I aimed for a wide variety of examples across age, background and gender. However, you might have noticed there weren't many female examples. And even though I tried to give you illustrations from across the world, I haven't covered any examples from Asia, from where there are many magnificent success stories and equally spectacular financial blunders. I hope to remedy some of the shortcomings of this book in future updates and extensions.

**My Mission**

My self-proclaimed mission is to convince more of you to develop an enlightened view on investing that goes beyond Wall Street, mutual funds, and your favorite financial website. I want you to protect yourself from an overhyped and, frankly, corrupt system that exorbitantly profits the few and takes without remorse from many. I want you to be financially self-sustaining and free of an unfavorably skewed system, by continuously studying the topics of entrepreneurship, investing and financial management. Don't aim for the shortcuts of Wall Street!

Today, I have created my own cash engines, e.g. writing books, providing consulting services, and investing in opportunities I enjoy an edge. I will be able to maintain this platform beyond any arbitrary retirement age and any adverse economic cycles. I am not dependent on market prices for my financial future. Yet, I still occasionally trade the markets and make use of financial markets to my benefit. I operate from a basis of financial strength, and I dictate the terms of what I buy or sell and when I do it. I trade when markets offer me outstanding opportunities with much higher return expectations and higher odds of winning, based on my personal edge. I encourage you to also aim for creating something that brings you financial freedom, fulfills you, and endures.

To encourage positive action for those who are committed to studying investing, and to continuously provide motivation and inspiration to develop and improve your personal investment approach, I maintain a website for individual and professional investors. To become a member of a growing tribe of 80/20 Investors, just subscribe at:

www.8020investors.com

I recommend posting your questions or comments about any topic covered in this book in our dedicated forum, or exclusive Facebook Group. Discuss your ideas or concerns with other like-minded investors. Gain insights into the world of investing, and begin your journey to financial freedom. I wish you all success on your investing journey,

David Woo Schneider

### *Get Your Bonus Chapter*

If you are interested in reading the bonus chapter about Middle Eastern wealth and blunders, subscribe to my email list. You will receive my bonus chapter that will cover two more examples from the Middle East: Prince Al-Waleed bin Talal and Muammar Qaddafi. Two biographies from the mystical Orient, and vast riches alongside blunders that rival one thousand and one nights.

*https://members.8020investors.com/pl/39848*

*Use the QR Code below to get to the download link!*

# Thank You

Before you go, I'd like to say "thank you" for purchasing this book.

These days, we are flooded with free content and investment guides that promise the world. So, a big thanks for downloading this book and reading all the way to the end. If you liked what you've read, then I need your help. Please take a moment to leave a review for this book.

**Amazon.com Review Link:**
https://www.amazon.com/review/create-review?asin=B07H7Q266X

Let others know that this book has quality and value for readers interested in this subject.

Thank you.

**David Woo Schneider**

# Acknowledgements

I would like to thank my launch team and all the people who reviewed and critiqued this book.

Special thanks to my research and editorial team. My editor, Valerie Smith, has been a great help in structuring the book and keeping deadlines. She is always the critical voice and eye of the team. I am grateful to my production team, which encompasses designers, researchers, a narrator, proofreaders, and many more.

I would like to thank my numerous friends from the DC community, my mastermind groups, as well as my sources and contacts in the financial industry who have always offered a helping hand and their personal views.

As always, I am grateful to my parents. They gave me all the opportunities a son could wish for, and which have allowed me to explore the world.

# About the Author

DAVID SCHNEIDER is the author of the bestselling The 80/20 Investor. He bought his first stock in 1994 at age 18.

Subsequently, he trained as a commercial banker, research analyst and investment manager. He developed a bottom-up value approach for selecting investment opportunities and managing concentrated portfolios based on the 80/20 principle.

Since 2011, David has been an independent investor, researcher, and writer. On his personal branding site, www.WooSchneider.com, he covers topics including wealth management, financial markets and investment opportunities around the world.

**Get in Touch:**

Twitter: @wooschneider
LinkedIn: *https://jp.linkedin.com/in/WooSchneider*
E-mail: *info@thewritingale.com*

# More from the Author

*The 80/20 Investor: Investing in an Uncertain and Complex World*

"Are you ready to set yourself free?" The 80/20 Investor, harnessing the power of the 80/20 principle, simplifies investing. In no time, you will learn where to look for "no-brainer" opportunities, find out how to finance your investment opportunities and minimize risks. This book allows you enter the seemingly intimidating world of investing, with valuable tips from some of those who have changed the game: the Rothschilds, Hetty Green, J. Paul Getty, Henry Singleton, and others. Only with financial freedom can you live the life you want to lead. Let The 80/20 Investor show you the way.

*Modern Investing: Gambling in Disguise*

Modern Investing is an indispensable guide to becoming an independent investor, rather than giving in to forces that regularly turn us into gamblers or speculators. It covers the basics every investor needs to know to start a successful investment career free of manipulation and dependence on "experts." By understanding investment history and its core principles, and contrasting it to the gambling culture of today, predominant financial scams and the peculiarities of our financial-political complex, you will be able to draw your own conclusions. More importantly, you will realize what options you still possess to make logical and independent decisions.

With the knowledge garnered from this book, you will be able to avoid scams and Wall Street chicanery; and most importantly, you will be able to establish a base investment strategy that can outperform any professional money manager, without the conventional risks. Buy this book and become an independent investor.

### *Index Funds & ETFs: What They Are and How to Use Them*

Index Funds and ETFs have seen stratospheric growth since the collapse of 2008—benefitting from computerized trading and quantitative forms of investment management. No matter where you look, the gospel of index fund investing has been taken to heart by the media and the masses alike. But what is the truth? How exactly do index funds work? Are they really the sure bet they're made out to be? This book will offer a different perspective—one that takes into account the history, structuring, and theorizing behind index funds and ETFs, and lay bare the inner workings of the industry.

---

# Notes

1 Bloomberg. "This Basically Anonymous Fund Manager Oversees $800 Billion." Accessed February 28, 2017.

2 Wasik, John F. Keynes's Way to Wealth: Timeless Investment Lessons from The Great Economist. McGraw-Hill Education. Kindle Edition.

3 Wasik

4 During his short stint as a civil servant at the India Office he would work on a book on the mathematical topic of probability. This was a book he researched and finished at Cambridge. It would eventually be published under the title Treatise on Probability, eventually hitting the shelves in 1921.

5 Roy Harrod, The Life of John Maynard Keynes (New York: Harcourt Brace, 1951), p. 163.

6 Wasik, John F. Keynes's Way to Wealth: Timeless Investment Lessons from The Great Economist (Kindle Locations 523-526). McGraw-Hill Education. Kindle Edition.

7 Liz Hoggard (21 October 2008). "Ten things you didn't know about Keynes". Evening Standard. UK. Keynes, John Maynard (1956). James R. Newman, ed. The World of Mathematics (2000 ed.). Dover. p. 277.

8 Harrod, Roy. The Life of John Maynard Keynes, Paperback (1983). W. W. Norton & Company.

9 Wasik

10 Skidelsky, Robert , accessed September, 2018, www.res.org.uk

11 Wasik

12 Wasik

13 Donald Moggridge, Maynard Keynes: An Economist's Biography (Routledge; 1 edition, 1995), 351.

14 Harrod

15 Harrod

16 Gilbert, Martin (2001). Churchill: A Study in Greatness (one-volume edition). London: Pimlico.

17 Lough, David (2015): No More Champagne: Churchill And His Money. USA: Picador.

18 UK Consumer Price Index inflation figures are based on data from Gregory Clark (2016), "The Annual RPI and Average Earnings for Britain, 1209 to Present (New Series)", MeasuringWorth.com.

19 Cohen, D. (2016, January/February). Why Winston Churchill Was So Bad With Money. The British prime minister could handle the Blitz but not his bills. Retrieved from https://www.theatlantic.com

20 Shakespeare, N. (2015, November 7). The truth behind Churchill's debts and reckless gambling. Retrieved from http://www.telegraph.co.uk

21 Lough, David (2015): No More Champagne: Churchill And His Money. USA: Picador.

22 Lough (2015)

23 Lough (2015)

24 Lough (2015)

25 Lough (2015)

26 Shakespeare (2015)

27 Shakespeare (2015)

28 Shakespeare (2015)

29 Shakespeare (2015)

30 Bensusan-Butt, 1980, accessed September, 2018, https://www.independent.co.uk/news/people/obituary-david-bensusan-butt-1367970.html

31 The Economist. The IMF in Britain: Toothless truth tellers, 2013.

32 "Jennifer Lawrence Net Worth," TheRichest, accessed September, 2018, https://www.therichest.com/celebnetworth/celeb/actress/jennifer-lawrence-net-worth/

33 "Spotting of Lawrence Talent," BusinessInsider, accessed September, 2018, http://www.businessinsider.com/jennifer-lawrence-bio-2016-8?IR=T/#and-after-all-this-shes-still-ranked-no-1-on-forbes-list-of-the-worlds-highest-paid-actresses-though-in-2016-she-earned-a-little-less-with-46-million-32

34 "Biography," thefamouspeople.com, accessed September, 2018,https://www.thefamouspeople.com/profiles/jennifer-lawrence-29821.php

35 "Jennifer Lawrence," Spectrum, accessed September, 2018,

https://twcc.com/entertainment/galleries/celebrity/jennifer-lawrence

36 "Jennifer Lawrence," Career Earnings Statistics, accessed September, 2018, http://www.statisticbrain.com/jennifer-lawrence-acting-career-earnings/

37 "Jennifer Lawrence Is Surprisingly Frugal," BusinessInsider, accessed September, 2018, https://www.businessinsider.com/jennifer-lawrence-is-surprisingly-frugal-2014-11?IR=T

38 "Mockingjay Star Jennifer Lawrence knows how to manage money," The Inquirer, accessed September, 2018, http://www.philly.com/philly/business/personal_finance/Mockingjay_Star_Jennifer_Lawrence_knows_how_to_manage_money.html

39 "Jennifer Lawrence on equal pay and why she's scared of death," News Australia, accessed September, 2018, https://www.news.com.au/entertainment/movies/new-movies/jennifer-lawrence-on-equal-pay-and-why-shes-scared-of-death/news-story/8ea92c1cd974599dea61243e81543e7a

40 "Jennifer Lawrence's Dating History — and What She's Said About Romance," People, accessed September, 2018, https://people.com/movies/jennifer-lawrence-dating-history-what-shes-said-about-romance/

41 "Johnny Depp's Bio," Biography, accessed September 2018, http://www.biography.com/people/johnny-depp-9542522

42 Total Earnings Statistics," Statisticbrain, accessed September, 2018, http://www.statisticbrain.com/johnny-depp-movie-career-statistics/

43 "A guide to Johnny Depp's 'extravagant and extreme' $2 million-a-month lifestyle," BusinessInsider, accessed September, 2018, http://www.businessinsider.com/how-johnny-depp-spends-his-money-2017-2?IR=T/#and-if-thats-not-enough-he-allegedly-has-55000-still-owing-on-a-visa-card-13

44 "Divorce Settlement," Daily Mail, accessed September, 2018, http://www.dailymail.co.uk/news/article-3742557/Johnny-Depp-Amber-Heard-

reach-settlement-close-10million-acrimonious-divorce-Hollywood.html

45 "Johnny Depp sues ex-managers alleging millions in losses," Fox News, accessed September, 2018, http://www.foxnews.com/entertainment/2017/01/14/johnny-depp-sues-ex-managers-alleging-millions-in-losses.html

46 "LeBron James' Net Worth as He Joins the Lakers," Go BankingRates, accessed September, 2018, https://www.gobankingrates.com/personal-finance/lebron-james-net-worth/

47 "LeBron James Tops The NBA's Highest-Paid Players 2016," Forbes Magazine, accessed September, 2018, https://www.forbes.com/sites/kurtbadenhausen/2016/01/20/lebron-james-tops-the-nbas-highest-paid-players-2016/#6a441db04508

48 "The Economics of LeBron's Homecoming," MacNicol & Associates, accessed September, 2018, http://macnicolasset.com/the-economics-of-lebrons-homecoming/#.WM5YEig3mM8

49 "The pizza chain backed by LeBron James just tripled sales," Business Insider, accessed September, 2018, http://www.businessinsider.com/blaze-pizza-tripled-its-sales-2016-3?IR=T

50 "Here's how Warren Buffett told LeBron James to invest his millions," John Szramiak, Vintage Value Investing, accessed September, 2018, https://www.businessinsider.com/warren-buffett-investing-advice-lebron-james-2016-6

51 "The Incredibly Smart Things LeBron James Has Done With His Money," Fool.com, accessed September, 2018, https://www.fool.com/investing/general/2014/10/12/the-incredibly-smart-things-lebron-james-has-don-2.aspx, http://www.businessinsider.com/warren-buffett-investing-advice-lebron-james-2016-6?IR=T

52 "LEBRON JAMES: How the king of the NBA spends his millions," Business Insider, accessed September, 2018, http://www.businessinsider.com/how-lebron-spends-his-money-2015-12?IR=T/#he-makes-around-44-million-per-year--nearly-twice-his-nba-salary--in-endorsements-2

53 "Maverick Carter, Founder of LRMR Innovative Marketing & Branding," Inc.com, accessed September, 2018, http://www.inc.com/30under30/2010/profile-maverick-carter-lrmr-innovative-marketing-branding.html

54 Fish, Mike, "The doctor they call 'Healing," ESPN, accessed September, 2018, http://www.espn.com/espn/otl/story/_/id/7324261/germany-dr-hans-wilhelm-muller-wohlfahrta-great-healer-quack-hyperactive-syringe

55 ESPN

56 PromiArzt in Schwierigkeiten: Mulls Wunden, Der Spiegel Magazin, accessed September, 2018, http://www.spiegel.de/sport/sonst/arzt-mueller-wohlfahrt-steckt-geschaeftlich-in-schwierigkeiten-a-1110765.html

57 Der Spiegel

58 Der Spiegel

59 Der Spiegel

60 Bunte Magazin, Betrug an der Ehefrau des Bayern-Docs, Spiegel Magazin, https://www.bunte.de/karin-mueller-wohlfahrt-betrug-der-ehefrau-des-bayern-docs-60262.html

61 Bunte Magazine: Seine Frau: „Unser ganzes Lebenswerk ist zerstört,", Spiegel Magazin, https://www.bunte.de/sport/hans-wilhelm-mueller-wohlfahrt-seine-frau-unser-ganzes-lebenswerk-ist-zerstoert-120252.html

62 "Profile: Carlos Slim," The Telegraph, accessed September, 2018, https://www.telegraph.co.uk/news/newstopics/profiles/4317646/Profile-Carlos-Slim.html

63 "Carlos Slim Biography," TheFamousPeople, accessed September, 2018, https://www.thefamouspeople.com/profiles/carlos-slim-5531.php

64 "Carlos Slim becomes top New York Times shareholder," Reuters, accessed September, 2018, https://www.reuters.com/article/us-new-york-times-warrants-carlos-slim-idUSKBN0KN2M820150114

65 "Mexico's Slim Buys 6.4% Stake in The Times Co," DealBook, accessed September, 2018, https://dealbook.nytimes.com/2008/09/10/mexicos-slim-buys-64-stake-in-the-times-co/

66 Grillo, IOAN, "Carlos Slim Secret Life," Time Magazine, accessed September, 2018, http://time.com/4132272/carlos-slim-secret-life/

67 Osorno, Time Magazine

68 "Eike Batista," Famous Entrepreneurs, accessed September, 2018, http://www.famous-entrepreneurs.com/eike-batista

69 ELLSWORTH, Brian. "The Billionaire from Brazil," Rio De Janeiro, December 2011.

70 "The salesman of Brazil," The Economist, accessed September, 2018, http://www.economist.com/node/21555907

71 Brazilian Private Equity: A New Direction, PWC, Insead, 2014 https://www.pwc.com.br/pt/publicacoes/setores-atividade/assets/private-equity/2014/pwc-insead-brazilian-private-equity-2014.pdf

72 "Big Man In Brazil," Forbes Magazine, accessed September, 2018, https://www.forbes.com/forbes/2010/0329/billionaires-2010-americas-brazil-eike-batista-big-man-in-brazil.html#77516a2218ec

73 Ellsworth, Brian. http://www.reuters.com/article/us-brazil-batista-idUSTRE7BG0BH20111217

74 "From billions to bust: where did it go wrong for Eike Batista?," World Finance, accessed September, 2018, http://www.worldfinance.com/markets/from-billions-

to-bust-where-did-it-go-wrong-for-eike-batista

75 "Eike Batista's fall from grace," FT.com, accessed September, 2018, https://www.ft.com/content/e5e78678-cd66-11e4-9144-00144feab7de

76 "Mikhail Prokhorov," Bloomberg Billionaires Index, accessed September, 2018, https://www.bloomberg.com/billionaires/profiles/mikhail-prokhorov/

77 "Rusal Agrees to Acquire 25% Stake in Norilsk," The Wall Street Journal, accessed September, 2018, https://www.wsj.com/articles/SB119603068939703344

78 "Profit of Norilsk Nickel," Statista, accessed September, 2018, https://www.statista.com/statistics/533179/profit-of-norilsk-nickel/

79 "Norilsk Nickel," Financial Times, accessed September, 2018, https://www.ft.com/content/be02ef20-132d-11e8-8cb6-b9ccc4c4dbbb

80 Financial Times

81 "How A Private Jet Full Of Prostitutes Saved Mikhail Prokhorov $10 Billion," Celebrity Networth, accessed September, 2018, http://www.celebritynetworth.com/articles/entertainment-articles/how-a-private-jet-full-of-prostitutes-saved-mikhail-prokhorov-10-billion/

82 Potanin announced the intent to acquire Prokhorov's Norilsk Nickel assets for a reported $1 billion.[16] Prokhorov offered to sell his 25% stake for $15 billion.[15] However, Potanin refused the deal and it never came to pass.

83 "Richest Russian's Newest Toy: An N.B.A. Team", The New York Times, accessed September, 2018, https://www.nytimes.com/2009/09/24/sports/basketball/24nets.html

84 "Russian Billionaire Buys NBA's Nets," Business Insider, accessed September, 2018, http://www.businessinsider.com/russian-billionaire-buys-nbas-nets-2009-9

85 who was rumored to be in dire financial conditions due to the aftermath of the subprime crisis.

86 estimated to be worth $10.7 billion in 2017

87 Bloomberg

88 The New York Times

89 "Barclays Center, which will continue to be wholly owned by (Prokhorov's) Onexim Sports and Entertainment."
https://www.cityandstateny.com/articles/opinion/commentary/mikhail-prokhorov-doesnt-own-barclays-center.html.

90 "Deripaska Rebound From Near-Crash Stares Down Potanin," Bloomberg, accessed September, 2018, https://www.bloomberg.com/news/articles/2011-02-21/deripaska-rebounding-from-near-disaster-stares-down-potanin-as-metals-soar

91 Bloomberg

92 Bloomberg

93 Bloomberg

94 Deripaska controlled Siberian Aluminum and the Chernoi brothers Trans World, Krasnoyarsk Aluminium and Bratsk Aluminium, key smelters in Russia.

95 Bloomberg

96 "The deal that made a Russian oligarch," The Guardian, accessed September, 2018, https://www.theguardian.com/business/2003/jul/06/russia.football

97 Bloomberg

98 "Deripaska Putin agreement signing," BBC, accessed September, 2018, https://www.youtube.com/watch?v=0XfbWnDXCx8

99 "Deripaska pins hopes on UK Tory peer to save EN+ and Rusal," Financial Times, accessed September, 2018, https://www.ft.com/content/36d6c364-4b95-11e8-97e4-13afc22d86d4

100 Trading in En+ global depositary receipts was suspended by UK regulators

101 Financial Times

102 Business insiders http://www.businessinsider.com/who-is-eike-batista-2013-2#also-this-private-jet-14

103 He defrauded, bankers, actors, to athletes, politicians and even European aristocrats

104 https://www.merriam-webster.com

105 https://www.psychologytoday.com/intl/blog/science-choice/201708/the-many-ways-we-lie-ourselves

106 Lough.

107 https://www.cnbc.com/2017/03/16/jay-lenos-brilliant-money-saving-strategy-is-something-anyone-can-try.html

108 Merriam-Webster, unforced error, accessed July 2017 https://www.merriam-webster.com/dictionary/unforced%20error.

109 LeBron James, Business Insider.

110 Business Insider.

111 "Warren Buffett's advice to LeBron James," CNBC, accessed September, 2018, https://www.cnbc.com/2015/03/02/warren-buffetts-advice-to-lebron-james.html

www.ingramcontent.com/pod-product-compliance
Lightning Source LLC
Chambersburg PA
CBHW071538220526
45469CB00003B/831